AAT TEXTBOOK

Intermediate (NVQ Level 3)
Unit 7

Preparing Reports and Returns

ISBN 1 84390 074 2

British Library Cataloguing-in-Publication data

A catalogue record for this book is available from the British Library.

We are grateful to the Association of Accounting Technicians for permission to reproduce past assessment materials. The solutions have been prepared by The Financial Training Company.

Published by

The Financial Training Company
22J Wincombe Business Park
Shaftesbury
Dorset
SP7 9QJ

Contents

Preface

This textbook has been specifically written for Unit 7 (Preparing Reports and Returns) of the AAT's Intermediate syllabus (NVQ Level 3).

The textbook is written in a practical and interactive style:

   ♦   key terms and concepts are clearly defined

   ♦   all topics are illustrated with practical examples with clearly worked solutions

   ♦   frequent practice activities throughout the chapters ensure that what you have learnt is regularly reinforced

   ♦   'pitfalls' and 'assessment tips' help you avoid commonly made mistakes and help you focus on what is required to perform well in your assessment.

Icons

Throughout the text we use symbols to highlight the elements referred to above.

   Key facts

   Assessment tips and techniques

   Pitfalls

   Practice activities

Syllabus

Unit 7   Preparing Reports and Returns

Unit commentary

What is the unit about?

This unit relates to the preparation of reports and returns from information obtained from all relevant sources The candidate is required to calculate ratios and performance indicators and present the information according to the appropriate conventions and definitions to either management or outside agencies, including the VAT office. The unit is also concerned with the communication responsibilities of the candidate which include obtaining authorisation before despatching reports, seeking guidance from the VAT office and presenting reports and returns in the appropriate manner.

Elements contained within this unit are:

Element 7.1   Prepare and Present Periodic Performance Reports

Element 7.2   Prepare Reports and Returns for Outside Agencies

Element 7.3   Prepare VAT Returns

Knowledge and Understanding

The Business Environment:

		Chapter
♦	Main sources of relevant government statistics (Elements 7.1 & 7.2)	1
♦	Awareness of relevant performance and quality measures (Element 7.1)	5
♦	Main types of outside organisations requiring reports and returns: regulatory; grant awarding; information collecting; trade associations (Element 7.2)	5, 6
♦	Basic law and practice relating to all issues covered in the range statement and referred to in the performance criteria Specific issues include: the classification of types of supply; registration requirements; the form of VAT invoices; tax points (Element 7.3)	7
♦	Sources of information on VAT: Customs and Excise Guide (Element 7.3)	7
♦	Administration of VAT: enforcement (Element 7.3)	7
♦	Special schemes: annual accounting; cash accounting; bad debt relief (Element 7.3)	7, 9

Accounting Techniques:

		Chapter
♦	Use of standard units of inputs and outputs (Elements 7.1 & 7.3)	5
♦	Time series analysis (Element 7.1)	4
♦	Use of index numbers (Element 7.1)	4
♦	Main types of performance indicators: productivity; cost per unit; resource utilisation; profitability (Elements 7.1 & 7.2)	6
♦	Ratios: gross profit margin; net profit margin; return on capital employed (Elements 7.1 & 7.2)	5, 6
♦	Tabulation of accounting and other quantitative information (Elements 7.1 & 7.2)	3
♦	Methods of presenting information: written reports; diagrammatic; tabular (Elements 7.1 & 7.2)	2, 3

The Organisation:

	Chapter
♦ Understanding of the ways the accounting systems of an organisation are affected by its organisational structure, its administrative systems and procedures and the nature of its business transactions (Elements 7.1, 7.2 & 7.3)	1
♦ Understanding of the purpose and structure of reporting systems with the organisation (Element 7.1)	1
♦ Background understanding that a variety of outside agencies may require reports and returns from organisations and that these requirements must be built into administrative and accounting systems and procedures (Elements 7.2 & 7.3)	1, 6
♦ Background understanding that recording and accounting practices may vary between organisations and different parts of organisations (Elements 7.1, 7.2 & 7.3)	Throughout
♦ An understanding of the basis of the relationship between the organisation and the VAT office (Element 7.3)	7, 9

Element 7.1   Prepare and present periodic performance reports

Performance criteria

		Chapter(s)
(i)	Information derived from different units of the organisation is consolidated into the appropriate form.	5
(ii)	Information derived from different information systems within the organisation is correctly reconciled.	5
(iii)	When comparing results over time an appropriate method, which allows for changing price levels, is used.	4
(iv)	Transactions between separate units of the organisation are accounted for in accordance with the organisation's procedures.	5
(v)	Ratios and performance indicators are accurately calculated in accordance with the organisation's procedures.	5
(vi)	Reports are prepared in the appropriate form and presented to management within required timescales.	2, 3

Range statement

1   Information: costs; revenue
2   Ratios: gross profit margin; net profit margin; return on capital employed
3   Performance indicators: productivity; cost per unit; resource utilisation; profitability
4   Methods of presenting information: written report containing diagrams; table

Evidence requirements

♦   Competence must be demonstrated consistently, over an appropriate timescale with evidence of performance being provided of periodic performance reports

Sources of evidence (These are examples of sources of evidence, but candidates and assessors may be able to identify other appropriate sources)

♦   Observed performance, eg

- Consolidating information in the appropriate form

- Reconciling information from different information systems

- Comparing results over time

- Calculating ratios and performance indicators

- Preparing reports

- Oral presentation of periodic performance reports

♦ Work produced by the candidate, eg

- Periodic performance reports containing written information, charts and graphs

- Calculations of ratios and performance indicators

- Correspondence between different units of the organisation

♦ Authenticated testimonies from relevant witnesses

♦ Personal accounts of competence, eg

- Report of performance

♦ Other sources of evidence to prove competence or knowledge and understanding where it is not apparent from performance, eg

- Performance in independent assessment

- Performance in simulation

- Responses to verbal questioning

Element 7.2   Prepare reports and returns for outside agencies

Performance criteria

		Chapter(s)
(i)	Relevant information is identified, collated and presented in accordance with the conventions and definitions used by outside agencies.	6
(ii)	Calculations of ratios and performance indicators are accurate.	5, 6
(iii)	Authorisation for the despatch of completed reports and returns is sought from the appropriate person.	6
(iv)	Reports and returns are presented in accordance with outside agencies' requirements and deadlines.	6

Range statement

1   Ratios: gross profit margin; net profit margin; return on capital employed

2   Reports and returns: written report; return on standard form

Evidence requirements

♦ Competence must be demonstrated consistently, over an appropriate timescale with evidence of performance being provided of reports and returns being presented to outside agencies

Sources of evidence (These are examples of sources of evidence, but candidates and assessors may be able to identify other appropriate sources)

♦ Observed performance, eg

- Collating information

- Presenting information

- Preparing reports and returns

- Calculating ratios and performance indicators

- Seeking authorisation for the despatch of reports and returns

- Work products produced by the candidate, eg

  - Written reports
  - Standard returns
  - Authorisation for despatch
  - Calculations of ratios and performance indicators
  - Correspondence with outside agencies

- Authenticated testimonies from relevant witnesses

- Personal accounts of competence, eg

  - Report of performance

- Other sources of evidence to prove competence or knowledge and understanding where it is not apparent from performance, eg

  - Reports and working papers
  - Performance in independent assessment
  - Performance in simulation
  - Responses to questions

Element 7.3   Prepare VAT returns

Performance criteria

		Chapter(s)
(i)	VAT returns are correctly completed using data from the appropriate recording systems and are submitted within the statutory time limits.	9
(ii)	Relevant inputs and outputs are correctly identified and calculated.	8
(iii)	Submissions are made in accordance with current legislation.	9
(iv)	Guidance is sought from the VAT office when required, in a professional manner.	7, 9

Range statement

1   Recording systems: computerised ledgers; manual control account; cash book

2   Inputs and outputs: standard supplies; exempt supplies; zero rated supplies; imports; exports

Evidence requirements

- Competence must be demonstrated consistently, with evidence of performance being provided of VAT returns with backup documentary evidence

Sources of evidence (These are examples of sources of evidence, but candidates and assessors may be able to identify other appropriate sources)

- Observed performance, eg

  - Completing VAT returns
  - Calculating inputs and outputs
  - Seeking guidance from the VAT office

- Work products, eg

  - Completed VAT returns
  - Calculations of inputs and outputs
  - Records of communications with the VAT office

- Authenticated testimonies from relevant witnesses

- Personal accounts of competence, eg

  - Report of performance

- Other sources of evidence to prove competence or knowledge and understanding where it is not apparent from performance, eg

  - Performance in simulation
  - Performance in independent assessment
  - Responses to questions

CHAPTER 1

Internal and external reporting

ASSESSMENT FOCUS

In assessments you may be required to prepare a report for internal management purposes or for some external agency.

This chapter covers the following Knowledge and Understanding and Performance Criteria of the AAT Syllabus.

> Main sources of relevant government statistics (*Knowledge and Understanding elements 7.1, 7.2*)
>
> Understanding of the ways the accounting systems of an organisation are affected by its organisational structure, its administrative systems and procedures and the nature of its business transactions (*Knowledge and Understanding elements 7.1, 7.2, 7.3*)
>
> Understanding of the purpose and structure of reporting systems within the organisation (*Knowledge and Understanding element 7.1*)
>
> Background understanding that recording and accounting practices may vary between organisations and different parts of organisations (*Knowledge and Understanding elements 7.2, 7.3*)

In order to cover these the following topics are included.

> The factors which will affect the internal information systems of an organisation
>
> Internal reporting of management information
>
> External reports and returns
>
> The differences between data and information
>
> Internal sources of data
>
> Primary and secondary data
>
> External sources of secondary data

1 Internal information systems

1.1 Introduction

A large amount of the data and information for preparation of reports will be **produced within the organisation itself**, from its accounting and administrative systems.

The exact format of the organisation's systems will depend upon its business, its objectives and its structure.

 An organisation's size, type of business, objectives and structure will have an impact on its internal information systems.

1.2   Size of business

A small 'corner shop' type of business will have fairly **basic** reporting requirements. The management and ownership of such a business are likely to overlap and there will be little need for formal internal reports.

The main source of information concerning the business that will satisfy both internal and external requirements will generally be the **financial accounts**, probably supported by a cash flow statement. The accounting system may thus consist mainly of cash records and files of invoices and other source documents.

Larger businesses will have a more defined management structure and will often be organised into **separate operating units for reporting purposes** (by different products/services or geographical location, for example). It is likely to have a greater demand for reporting to external parties such as investors, tax and government authorities, regulatory bodies (eg the Stock Exchange) and trade associations. Thus its accounting and administrative systems need to be more sophisticated to cope with the range of both internal and external information needs; these systems are invariably computer-based.

1.3   Type of organisation – objectives

An organisation may be **private sector** or **public sector**, both of which have different objectives and reporting requirements.

Definition   A **public sector** enterprise is owned and funded by central or local government – for example, hospitals, libraries, schools, etc.

They are generally run to provide services rather than to make a profit. Their information systems will thus be geared towards recording and reporting on expenditure levels and productivity/efficiency measures.

Definition   A **private sector** business is owned and funded by individual investors.

It may be a sole trader, partnership or limited company and will generally be profit-seeking to give a return to its investors. **Charities** are a typical example of the exception to this. Reporting requirements will primarily focus upon **revenue, cost and profit information**, although secondary objectives – such as staff development, product innovation, increasing market share and environmental considerations – will also affect the design of information systems.

Externally, companies (particularly public limited companies), will be required to provide quite **extensive information** and the systems must also be able to cope with these demands.

1.4   Type of business

Businesses can generally be categorised into retailers, manufacturers and service organisations.

Manufacturers and retailers will deal with distinct products, for which detailed unit cost and revenue information will be required for internal control and decision-making.

Service organisations may keep records by client (accountants, solicitors), by department (hospitals, schools, etc.) or by location/branch (estate agents, restaurants). Employee time will be an important feature of costing; pricing and efficiency reports and systems will need to incorporate timesheet and charge-out aspects.

1.5 The organisational structure

A **profit-seeking manufacturing business** is used here for illustration purposes, although the general principles can be applied to all types of business.

Such a business may be organised along the following lines.

(a) A **chief executive** and **main board** are appointed who have overall control of the business unit. They are responsible for achieving the stated objectives and are answerable to the providers of funds (eg the shareholders).

(b) The chief executive/board may appoint certain **key managers** who take responsibility for the various management functions of:

    (i) finance;

    (ii) marketing;

    (iii) production;

    (iv) personnel.

(c) These key managers may further **delegate responsibility** within their functional areas for certain activities.

1.6 Organisation chart

The organisational structure of a business is often illustrated in an organisation chart.

Chief executive/Main board

Finance	Marketing	Production	Personnel
	Press office Sales office Sales managers	Buying Factory operations	
Management accounts Financial accounts			Staff records Welfare services

There is a sub-division of responsibilities between these areas, but in practical terms there is a considerable degree of **interdependence** between each functional area. However, each separate function can be described as a *system* and each *system* fits together to make up the whole organisation.

 This type of organisational structure is based upon the functions within the business.

1.7   Other organisational structures

Other structures may be according to:

◆   **Products/services** – The initial tier below the chief executive/main board is split according to the individual or groups of products or services offered by the business. Each of these will then be progressively split by function and/or geographical location.

◆   **Geographical region** – The initial tier is split by region (within the UK: North, South, etc or worldwide: Europe, America, Far East, etc.). Subsequent tiers may then be split by product, function, etc.

1.8   Effects of organisational structure on information systems

However an organisation is initially structured, all will have the common functional elements as illustrated by the above chart. These will deal with the **basic recording, processing and analysing of the business's transactions** and the production of financial and management accounts.

Organisations that are split at some level by **product/service** or **geographical region** will have additional requirements from their systems.

◆   **Product/service split**. The functional information will be grouped in such a way that revenue earned and costs incurred by particular products/services are separately identified. This causes particular problems on the cost side, where items of expenditure must be allocated between products/services. Suitable coding systems can be used for direct expenses (labour, materials, etc) but there will also need to be a system for splitting shared overheads between products/services.

◆   **Geographical split**. The main potential problems to deal with will involve international regions. Different currencies, legal and reporting requirements and business methods must be rationalised to produce information that is comparable and can be combined into reports on the organisation as a whole. Systems for areas such as pricing and performance measures may also be affected by **political, economic, social and market factors** which will impact upon a country's accounting practices.

2   Internal reports – management information

2.1   Management activity

Internal reports will form an important means of providing management information. Information will be provided for various purposes and at various levels, but will generally be tied in with one or more of the commonly defined areas of management activity:

◆   forecasting

◆   planning

◆   organising

◆   co-ordinating

◆   decision-taking

◆   controlling.

All these tasks are directed at the **achievement of corporate objectives** that were mentioned earlier. It also follows that, if these tasks are to be carried out, managers must have some system for communication, either with the outside world or within the business.

Managers need information in order to manage.

2.2   Information purposes

The information associated with managerial activities can be analysed as being needed for three purposes, often identified with **senior (ie strategic), middle (ie tactical)** and **shop-floor (ie operational)** management levels:

(a)   **Strategic level** – Information is needed on long-term plans and corporate objectives as well as strategies to improve the size of the organisation and ultimately the performance. Information will be drawn from both internal and external sources.

(b)   **Tactical level** – Information is needed for short-term decision-making and may be concerned with yearly production plans, forecasts of cash and sales analyses. Such information is typically internally generated and of a financial nature.

(c)   **Operational level** – Information is needed here for the day to day running of the business to ensure that the company's activities are carried out in an orderly and efficient manner. This will often be non-financial, relating to scheduling and other operational policies of the organisation.

2.3   Information levels

Most business organisations require information at various levels:

♦   **International** information, such as the state of commodity markets, relative strengths of currencies, and political affairs

♦   **National** information, such as government policies, trading conditions and the impact of new legislation

♦   **Corporate** information, such as business performance and financial results

♦   **Departmental** information, such as individual budgets for costs and actual expenditure compared therewith

♦   **Individual** information, such as sales made by individual salespersons and remuneration of individuals

2.4   Types of internal report to management

Management may require various types of reports for their various purposes:

♦   **Regular reports** – These are reports which relate to a cycle of activities (eg payroll processing and sales ledger processing).

♦   **Exception reports** – These are reports prepared to highlight some unusual occurrence and prompt the user to take corrective action (eg significant variances of costs from budget).

♦   **Analyses** – Analyses are items of data which are considered and commented on. Analysis may be done on a regular or on an ad hoc basis.

♦   **Forecasts** – Forecasts are merely the result of intelligent conjectures about the future based upon the past. Forecasting methods vary from naive methods to more advanced methods using mathematical models which attempt to simulate the degree of uncertainty that arises in business life.

2.5   Qualities of good information

What makes information of good quality?

- **Promptness** – The value of information declines with the length of time that the user has to wait for it. Information that is out of date is a waste of time, effort and money.

- **Brevity** – The information provided should concentrate on the essentials and ignore trivia. Too much information can blind the user to the truly important matters contained therein.

- **Accuracy** – Inaccurate information is of little use for strategic, tactical or operational purposes. The degree of accuracy of information will vary; the managing director may be concerned with the reporting of profit to the nearest thousand pounds. On the other hand the sales ledger supervisor will be concerned with a high degree of accuracy with regard to the balancing of the control account.

- **Discrimination** – Information should be tailored to the needs and level of understanding of the recipient. The degree of detail required by the credit controller to monitor the level of debt is different from the level of detail required by the chief executive.

- **Economy** – Information has no intrinsic value. Its value can only be gauged by the benefit that management obtain from its use. Information should not be produced wastefully. Only essential reports are produced which enable management to take effective action.

- **Capability for exception reporting** – The information system should be capable of highlighting the unusual so that appropriate action can be taken by the recipient.

Activity 1 *(The answer is in the final chapter of this book)*

Employment information (AAT CA D93)

An organisation has started to collect monthly information regarding employment and labour costs from its various departments. At the moment it only records average rates of pay in each department. Suggest three other items of management information that you believe should be collected relating to employment.

---

3   External reports and returns

3.1   Introduction

The second element of Unit 7 is concerned with the **preparation of reports and returns for outside agencies**. The accounting and other information systems of a business organisation must take the requirements of such agencies into account, as far as is practicable.

The main types of external organisations requiring reports and returns have been identified as **regulatory, grant awarding and information collecting**.

3.2   Regulatory organisations

- **Inland Revenue** – returns in relation to the employees' payroll (income tax deductions (PAYE) and National Insurance contributions (NIC)); corporation tax returns (companies)

- **Customs and Excise** – VAT returns (see the detail in later chapters)

- **Department of Trade and Industry** (DTI) – company financial statements

- **Health and Safety Executive, Training Commission, Local Authorities' Planning Departments** – often non-financial information regarding the operations, employment policies and plans of the business

- **Sector regulatory bodies** – financial service organisations, banks and listed companies are required to submit regular returns concerning their operations and finances to the appropriate regulatory body (eg FSA, The Bank of England and the Stock Exchange).

3.3 Grant awarding organisations

If a business wishes to take advantage of the various awards and grants available from government and privately funded schemes, it will need to support its application with certain information. Examples include the **Enterprise Initiative**, run by the DTI to offer grant, information and advisory assistance.

3.4 Information-collecting organisations

These agencies will **collect information for analysis for their own purposes** and for use by interested parties, including the organisations supplying the information.

Examples include the following.

- **Office for National Statistics** collects information for the compilation of reports on such topics as business statistics, consumer expenditure patterns and social trends.

- **Trade associations** conduct voluntary surveys of member businesses concerning wage levels, resource utilisation, key ratios, etc.

- **General market survey organisations**

3.5 Other external reporting requirements

As well as the requirements of the organisations discussed above, a business will need to cater for the information demands of external parties who have a particular interest in it. These will include **shareholders** (existing and potential), **customers and suppliers, banks, debenture-holders** and other lenders.

3.6 Problems of reporting for external agencies

Much of the information required for external reports and returns will be available from the normal accounting/administrative systems of the organisation (eg VAT, PAYE, NI information). However, some of the information required is **specialised** (financial statistics, non-financial data) which may or may not be part of the organisation's own management accounting requirements.

Thus there may be a need to set up **special data collecting exercises or routines** (computerised or manual) to pick up the relevant data and sort it as required by the particular report or return.

 Reporting to an external agency may require information that is not normally part of the management information of the organisation.

Activity 2 *(The answer is in the final chapter of this book)*

Agency return (AAT CA J93)

(a)   Give an example of a periodic report which has to be made to an outside agency by any organisation.

(b)   What is the main purpose of this return?

4   Sources of data for internal and external reports

4.1   Introduction

Most of the work involved in producing a report is in the initial stages of **collection and organisation of the required data and information.**

4.2   Data and information

The terms **data** and **information** are commonly used to mean the same thing, but it is important to distinguish between the two.

Definition   **Data** is raw facts, unassembled and frequently unrelated to one another.

Definition   **Raw data** is numerical information or figures that are initially collected together and noted down. This is before any kind of analysis is carried out on the figures. These figures are called *variables*.

Definition   **Information** is obtained by processing the data in some way. It can be defined as an organised collection of related pieces of data.

4.3   Variables

A **variable** is a measurement which varies from one individual to another or from one item to another. Examples of variables are the length of time a contract takes to fulfil, the number of mistakes in a set of accounts, the weight of a steel bar, the average age of a group of people and so on. Variables can be one of two types depending on what values they can take.

Definition   **Discrete variables** are those which can only take certain (typically integer) values. When items are counted, the answer is a whole number. Examples include the number of people who use a microcomputer in an hour and the number of cars sold in a day.

Definition   **Continuous variables** are variables which can take any value within a certain range, so a decimal or a fractional value can be obtained. Most physical measurements can take decimal values and so are continuous variables. Examples of these include the width of a component, temperature and time to produce an item.

4.4   Example

Are the following variables discrete or continuous?

(1)   Volume of a bottle

(2)   Number of bottles produced in a day

(3)   Number of people absent from work on a weekday

4.5   Solution

(1)   As volume can take decimal values, it is a continuous variable.

(2)   As this is a count of bottles, it will be a whole number and a discrete variable.

(3)   As this is also a count of people, it will be a discrete variable.

4.6   How data becomes information

Without some sort of analysis, **raw data can be rather unhelpful** since it is often impossible to see any trends in a mass of figures. In general data may be transformed into information in a number of ways:

♦   bringing related pieces of data together, ie. **grouping** data;

♦   **summarising** data;

♦   performing basic calculations, ie **processing** data;

♦   **tabulation** and diagrammatic techniques;

♦   **statistical analysis**;

♦   **financial analysis**.

 Statistical information is needed to run any business organisation. For example, planning future sales targets requires analysis of past sales data and calculating employees' wages requires analysis of data from clock cards. Managers will use available information to obtain the best results consistent with the objectives of the organisation.

The data from which the information is obtained may arise from **internal sources** and/or **external sources**.

4.7   Internal sources of data

Business organisations themselves produce **huge amounts of data**. For example:

(a)   There are 25 employees in the export department.

(b)   Last year's budget for the personnel department was £265,000.

(c)   In December 20X2, 1,500 type LA31 engines were produced.

(d)   Last month 358 expense claims were submitted.

These are all items of data internal to the organisation. Data produced within an organisation will obviously vary from organisation to organisation. For a 'typical' organisation, five **major activities** might be considered:

(1)   **Production** – amount of stock available, quality of goods produced, productivity, frequency of machine breakdowns;

(2)   **Marketing** – sales figures, expenditure on advertising and promotion, results from market research surveys, travelling expenditure by representatives;

(3)   **Purchasing** – price of raw materials, consumption of stationery, occurrence of overdue deliveries;

(4)   **Finance** – wage rates of employees, cash in hand, bad debt details, details of loans held;

(5)   **Administration** – number of employees, costs of maintenance, number of mailings.

4.8   External sources of data

Organisations frequently need to make use of **data obtained outside the organisation itself**. For example:

♦   a **survey** may be commissioned to determine customer satisfaction with service arrangements in a large store;

♦   data on the size and the characteristics of a **section of the population** may be useful to determine the number of potential customers for a product;

♦   if a company is to compete successfully, it will need details of the **activities of its competitors**.

5   Primary and secondary data

5.1   Introduction

Data can be categorised into **primary** and **secondary data**

Definition   Primary data is any data which is used solely for the purpose for which it was originally collected.

Definition   Secondary data is data that has already been collected for some other purpose but can also be used for the purpose in hand.

An important distinction is made here since information collected for one purpose by a business and then, at a later date, used again for another purpose would **no longer be primary data**.

5.2   Example

Decide which of the following are primary data and which are secondary data.

(a)   Information from clock cards when used for making up wages.

(b)   Data from a government publication on the toy industry used by a new toy shop to determine which items to stock.

(c)   Expense claim forms submitted by sales representatives used to estimate the car mileage they have travelled.

(d)   Results of an election opinion poll published in a newspaper.

5.3   Solution

(a)   Obviously this is primary data, since the data is collected to make up the wages.

(b)   This is secondary data; government statisticians collate data from various sources and the data is used in a variety of ways (see later in this chapter).

(c)   This is secondary data since the expense claim data is collected for a different reason initially.

(d)   This is primary data since the data was collected specifically for the purpose. If you said secondary data you were probably thinking that the results were being used to predict the result of the election; this is different from the reason why it was collected.

5.4   The problem of using secondary data

Primary data (if available) is preferable to secondary data since data collected for a specific purpose is likely to be **better** than data acquired for some other purpose. Some of the **problems with secondary data** are:

♦   **The data has been collected by someone else.** There is no control over how it was collected. If a survey was used, was a suitable questionnaire used? Was a large enough sample taken (was enough data collected)? Was it a reputable organisation that carried out the data collection?

♦   **Is the data up to date?** Data quickly becomes out of date, for example, people's consumer tastes change and prices may fluctuate wildly.

♦   **The data may be incomplete.** Certain groups of people are sometimes omitted from the published data. For example, do you know which groups are included in the unemployment figures?

♦   **What is the data?** Is it actual, seasonally adjusted, estimated or a projection?

♦   **The reason for collecting the data may be unknown.** Statistics published on motor cars may include or exclude three wheeled cars, vans and motor caravans. Readers need to know which categories are included in the data.

If secondary data is to be used, these questions need to be answered. Sometimes the answers will be published with the data itself or sometimes it may be possible to contact the people who collected the data. If not, users must be aware of the **limitations of making decisions based on information produced from secondary data.**

5.5   Sources of secondary data

Sources of secondary data are numerous and can be broadly categorised as of two forms – those produced by individual organisations and those produced by the government.

5.6   Data from individual organisations

Some examples of such data are:

Bank of England Quarterly Bulletin – reports on financial and economic matters.

Financial Times (daily) – share prices and information on business.

Company reports – information on performance and accounts of individual companies.

Labour Research – articles on industry, employment, political parties and trade unions.

South Yorkshire Statistics (annual) – a selection of statistics relevant to the area.

5.7   Government statistics

The **Office for National Statistics (ONS)** is a government agency which exists primarily to meet the needs of government. However, much of the information compiled is readily usable by business and other organisations. Since its creation in 1996 (from a number of other government agencies) the service to business has been extended and CD ROMs and books have been published which has encouraged businesses to make more use of government statistics.

The service works in the following way.

♦ Each government department prepares and publishes its own statistics via ONS outlets.

♦ If any series of data from these departments is of sufficient interest it is usually included in more general publications like the *Monthly Digest of Statistics.*

The ONS publishes an **extensive range of statistical digests**. To help find the publication most suitable to anyone's needs two useful guides are available:

♦ *Government Statistics* – a brief guide to sources, listing all the main publications and departmental contact points; and

♦ *Guide to Official Statistics* – a more comprehensive list.

Some of the more important digests are **general** and some more **specific**.

5.8   General digests

♦ *Monthly Digest of Statistics* – a collection of the main series of data from all government departments

♦ *Annual Abstract of Statistics* – similar to Monthly Digest but containing more series and over longer periods of time

♦ *Social Trends* – a collection of key social and demographic statistics, presented using charts and tables

5.9   Specific digests

♦ *Economic Trends* provides a background to trends in the UK economy.

♦ *British Business* contains statistics and commentary from the Department of Trade and Industry. The contents vary (weekly) but include statistics on capital expenditure, investment intentions, industrial production, company liquidity, acquisitions and insolvencies, regional development grants.

♦ *National Accounts* contains detailed estimates of national accounts, including consumer expenditure.

♦ *Overseas Trade Statistics of the UK* gives detailed statistics of exports and imports.

♦ *Employment Gazette* includes articles, tables and charts on manpower, employment, unemployment, earnings, labour costs and stoppages due to disputes.

♦ *New Earnings Survey* contains statistics relating to earnings from employment by industrial occupation and region.

♦ *Financial Statistics* contains key financial and monetary statistics for the UK.

♦ *Business Monitors* is a series of publications in which a wide variety of statistics are produced, examples of which are:

   (a) annual data relating to cinemas;

   (b) monthly data on road vehicles and new registrations;

(c) quarterly data on insurance companies and private pension funds;

(d) annual analysis of the accounts of listed and unlisted companies;

(e) monthly list of price indices for current cost accounting.

 If a business is to remain successful and competitive then it will need a wide variety of data about the environment within which it operates. Government statistics are a useful source of this data.

 **Activity 3** *(The answer is in the final chapter of this book)*

Employment Gazette (AAT CA D94 – amended)

A manufacturing company has a copy of the *Employment Gazette* which contains statistics relating to:

(a)   employment and unemployment;

(b)   earnings.

State to what practical purposes both (a) and (b) could be used by the company.

---

6 Summary

In this initial chapter consideration has been given to the general reporting requirements and systems of organisations. We have seen that the particular reporting system of an organisation will depend upon the size, nature and organisational structure of the organisation.

We then looked at the need for internal management information and the fact that in order to manage a business successfully information must be provided on the strategic, tactical and operational level. When providing information for management, it is also important that this is useful information which means that it must be prompt, accurate and understandable.

Information may also need to be provided to external agencies in the form of reports or returns. Such information must be accurate and also may not be the normal information provided by the internal management information system.

It is important to distinguish between data and information. Data is unanalysed facts whereas information is data which has been analysed in some way. Another important distinction is between primary and secondary data, the former being of more direct use and the latter requiring care with its use.

Finally the information made available by the government was considered. This vast array of information can be useful to most organisations in assessing their position within the UK market.

CHAPTER 2

Writing reports

ASSESSMENT FOCUS

In most assessments you will be required to prepare a report of some sort. Normally these will be fairly short informal reports but in practice you may be required to prepare longer more formal reports therefore all aspects will be covered in this chapter.

This chapter covers the following Knowledge and Understanding and Performance Criteria of the AAT Syllabus.

> Reports are prepared in the appropriate form and presented to management within required timescales *(Performance Criteria element 7.1)*

> Methods of presenting information: written reports; diagrammatic; tabular *(Knowledge and Understanding elements 7.1, 7.2)*

In order to cover these the following topics are included.

> A report as a means of effective business communication

> Simple reports in a memo, letter or short form report

> The structure of more formal reports

> An overview of writing a report

> Checks to make on a report once written

> Page layout and headings

> Language to use and not to use in a report

1 Reports as a means of effective business communication

1.1 Introduction

A **report** could be defined as an orderly and objective **communication of factual information** which serves some business aim. Its purpose is to convey information to particular readers or to answer a question.

Report is a general term. A letter containing specific information could be classified as a report or a memo drawing someone's attention to certain details could be classified as a report.

Reports do not even have to be written; it does happen that people are requested to, or offer to, make **oral reports**.

1.2   Purpose of a report

The object of a report is **communication**, not to show how much knowledge the writer possesses. Reports vary in length and status from simple printed forms (such as accident reports) to the major investigative reports commissioned by governments.

The prime reason for producing a report is to **save time (and thus money).** The further people rise up the promotional ladder within a firm or an organisation the more remuneration they receive and the more precious their time becomes. They have no time to do the research and investigation necessary before producing a report. Generally, someone else produces the report for their use. Furthermore, successful report-writers package the document in such a form that it can be quickly and easily read to ensure no more time is spent in reading the report than is absolutely necessary.

Another reason for producing written reports is to provide a **permanent source of reference**. Even a number of years after being produced a report might need to be consulted to solve a problem, to find out the details of an accident or to determine who recommended a certain course of action.

 By virtue of either their position or function within an organisation or their having discovered something or having been asked to investigate something, the writers of reports produce them to **convey information to people**.

1.3   Functions of a report

Reports have five different **functions** as follows:

♦   informing – gathering information

♦   analysing – analysing the information gathered

♦   evaluating – so the reader can make a decision based on the report

♦   recommending – recommendation of a future course of action

♦   describing – noting observations.

2   Structure of reports

2.1   Introduction

Reports can take **many forms** and can vary in length and status from:

(a)   **simple reports** in memo, letter or short report form; to

(b)   **fixed format reports**, such as accident reports; to

(c)   reports on **internal matters within a company** which may be formal or informal; to

(d)   **formal reports**, such as the findings of public enquiries.

2.2   Simple reports in memo, letter or short report form

Many written reports in industry are **simple reports** concerning day-to-day problems and these tend to be short and informal. As such, they have a short life and are intended for only a few readers who are familiar with the problem and its background. The reader will generally be interested in the findings of the report and any action it will lead to.

Of the conventional short forms of informal report, three in particular deserve special attention: **the short report**, the **letter report** and the **memorandum report**. These will vary widely in form and arrangement, depending on the purpose for which they have been written.

2.3   *The short informal report*

This is generally only a **two or three section report**. The main areas are:

(i)   the name of the person requesting the report;
(ii)   the title;
(iii)   an introduction, which may also give the background;
(iv)   the procedure, information, findings and 'overview' of the problem;
(v)   the conclusion;
(vi)   the name and position within the company of the writer; and
(vii)   the date.

The following example shows the basic structure but may be adapted to suit different requirements.

2.4   *Example of a short informal report*

To: D Fagen

Date: 29 July 20X6

Accounts Department reaction to proposed hot drinks vending machine installation

Introduction

This report describes the reaction of staff in the Accounts department of the Kenilworth branch office of Teck Bros to a proposal to replace existing tea and coffee-making arrangements with a hot drinks vending machine. The report was prepared on the instructions of D. Fagen, Branch Manager and written by J. Ely, Office Junior, Accounts Department. Instructions to prepare the report were received on 24 July 20X6 and it was submitted on 29 July 20X6.

Procedure

It was decided to interview personally all twelve members of staff in the Accounts Department. All staff were notified in advance. Questions were devised, three to establish staff reactions and a fourth inviting comments. All staff were then interviewed and the results noted. (A copy is appended to this report.)

Findings

(a)   In response to the question 'Would you be happy to see a vending machine installed?' EIGHT people said Yes, THREE said No and ONE was uncertain.

(b)   In response to the question 'Are you happy with the present arrangements?' THREE people said Yes, EIGHT people said No and ONE appeared unconcerned.

(c)   In response to the question 'Would you like to have a wider range of hot drinks available to you?' EIGHT people said Yes, THREE people said No and ONE was uncertain.

(d)   Amongst the comments made when staff were invited to comment on the proposal were 'Will fixed times for coffee and tea breaks disappear?' 'What about the tea ladies?' and 'I would prefer to obtain drinks at my own convenience'.

Conclusion

A clear majority of the staff (two-thirds) are in favour of this proposal.

J Ely
Office Junior
Accounts Department

2.5 *The letter report*

As the name implies this is a report written in **letter form**. It is used primarily to present information to or by someone outside the company. For example, an outside consultant may write his analysis and recommendations in the form of a letter, signing the letter as normal.

2.6 *Memorandum reports*

Memorandum reports are used primarily for routine reporting within an organisation, although some companies use them for external communicating. Because they are largely internal communications, they are often written on standardised inter-office memorandum stationery.

Following the company's identification or logo, if there is one, the words *From, To* and *Subject* appear at the top of the page. Sometimes the date is also part of the heading. Like letters, the memorandum may carry a signature or the writer may merely initial the heading.

2.7 *Example of a memorandum report*

The business supplies buyer of Datewise has asked one of his clerks to investigate the costs and supply of 108mm × 219mm white envelopes, with a view to finding a cheaper source.

Memorandum

To: Mr Hopkins

From: A Clerk   **Date:** 4 January 20X7

Subject: Supply of envelopes

As requested I have investigated the local suppliers of the 108mm × 219mm white envelopes and compared the costs.

There are three main office suppliers to choose from: Paper Products, Office Treasures and Bestbuy.

Our current supplier, Bestbuy, has free delivery and offers us a 25% discount on orders over £100.

Paper Products offer boxes of 1,000 envelopes £3 cheaper than Bestbuy on orders of six or more boxes. They offer the same discount and have a free delivery once a fortnight in this area. Special deliveries carry a charge of £20.

Office Treasures are the same price as Paper Products but, as we would be new customers, they will not discuss discounts.

Paper Products would be most suitable for us as we always order more than six boxes and rarely need special delivery. I would recommend them for future supplies of envelopes.

2.8 *Fixed format reports*

Some reports, such as **accident reports** and **personnel appraisal reports**, will be a fixed length and style because the report is a fixed format.

2.9   *Example of a fixed format report*

Vehicle accident report

Branch & reference .... Claim number ....

Important – Reports in respect of accidents to motor and electric vehicles should be forwarded to the Distribution Director no later than 24 hours after the accident has occurred.

PLEASE COMPLETE IN BLOCK CAPITALS

Date of accident....................Hour........................am/pm   Condition of road Wet or Dry

Driver's name.......................Age..Licence No ....

Address ....

State if person was injured ....

Place where accident occurred ....

Did you give any warning and how?...

What was the speed of your vehicle immediately before impact? ....

Company details	**Opposing vehicle or property (third party)**
Vehicle Reg No..	Description of opposing vehicle or property
Make	....
Damage to vehicle	Driver's name ....
Goods damaged, value as on ledger (attach a/c)	Address ....
....	....
Did police witness accident? Yes/No	Name & address of any injured third party
If so, officer's No. & Station	
....	....
Name of witness (1)..	Nature of injuries..
Address	Which hospital? ....
....	Damage to third party property...........................
Name of witness (2)..	....
Address	....
....	Third party insurers..

ON A SEPARATE SHEET DESCRIBE HOW THE ACCIDENT OCCURRED

3   Structure of formal reports

3.1   Introduction

Formal reports (such as the findings of public enquiries) may be internal or external to the organisation, and are used for the more complex and important investigations commissioned by senior management.

In general, they will include the following:

(a) **introduction**, including terms of reference and background to the report;

(b) **approach to the investigation**;

(c) detailed **findings** (some of which may be presented as an Appendix);

(d) **conclusions** and **recommendations**, as appropriate.

The findings of **public enquiries** are presented in terms of a formal report. In terms of length and style, these are likely to be the longest and most formal of reports.

 **Structure** is very important. The report will be used for reference so readers need to be able to find the information they need quickly and easily. Formal written reports usually contain the basic sections listed below, though there are often slight variations.

3.2 Title page

The title. This should give a good idea of what the report is about, without being too long. It should be easy to find in a filing system.

- The date of issue

- Circulation list (if appropriate)

- Name of author(s)

- Author's position and department

- Name and address of organisation

3.3 Summary or synopsis

The major **uses of summaries** are:

- to help readers decide whether to read the whole report;

- to enable readers to see the key points;

- to focus attention on the aim of the report.

Write the summary after the report is finished. As a rough guide, it should be about 10% of the length of the report and should only contain material included in the main report.

Include in the summary:

- a brief statement of the problem investigated;

- a summary of the main points, concentrating on the conclusion;

- an outline of any recommendations.

3.4 Table of contents

A list of **headings** and **sub-headings** and their page numbers. The contents page should provide an overview. The headings should be meaningful.

3.5 Introduction

Introduce and clearly state the main topic of the report. Give background factual information sufficient to 'set the scene', familiarise the reader with the context and prepare him for what is to follow. You may also be required to give terms of reference.

3.6 Main text

◆ A fuller statement of the problem.

◆ How it was investigated and what was discovered.

◆ Informative **headings** for each section and sub-section. A section may comprise one or more paragraphs, consisting of a main point, reasons and factual evidence.

3.7 Conclusions

(a) **Summarise** the key points made in the main body of the report and summarise findings, showing briefly but clearly how they are logically derived from the supporting evidence presented.

(b) **Evaluate the findings**, questioning whether they are a complete answer to the problem.

(c) **No new information** is to be included in the conclusions.

3.8 Recommendations

Recommendations, if required, can be included with the conclusions or treated separately.

(a) They should recommend a certain course of action in accordance with the conclusions reached.

(b) Any recommendations made should be prepared for in the main body, along with consideration of their viability.

3.9 Appendix

Appendices should be given informative headings and structured so that the reader can understand them. They should not include information which readers will need in order to follow the main text.

(a) Their use is to provide more detailed information which is of interest but either too technical or too peripheral for most readers of the report.

(b) This is also the place to provide documentation for facts presented in the report, eg. letters, faxes, tables, etc.

(c) Computer programs might be presented in the appendix.

3.10 Acknowledgements

These can be at the beginning or at the end if it is felt appropriate to **thank people**.

3.11 References

The **references** must contain a list of books, articles, etc. which have been consulted, if the report has required it. When referring to information from these sources in the body of the report, they must be acknowledged by means of a referencing system.

References need the following details:

♦ **Books**: Author, Title, Publisher, Edition (unless 1st), Place of publication, Date, Chapter, and page number if relevant.

♦ **Journals**: Author, Title, Journal, Volume, Number, date and page number if relevant.

3.12 Citing sources in the text

Make sure you have **factual evidence** to support your points, and that the reader can discover the source and date of this evidence. If your source is a book or journal it is usual to use a referencing system in the main text, which refers the reader to a section of references or a bibliography at the end of the report. There are several ways of doing this. One way is to number the references as they appear in the text, and then list them in the bibliography or references in the order in which they appear in the report.

It is important to use a **range of sources** and to be aware of any potential for bias or for unreliability in the source.

Your text should **essentially be your points and ideas** with supporting evidence obtained by research of some kind. If the source is a written one, then either the appropriate information can be paraphrased (put into your own words), or it can be quoted, using quotation marks, though the latter must be used sparingly.

In both cases the **source must be acknowledged**. The main body of the report should never consist of a long series of quotations or paraphrases with little or no text of your own.

4 Writing a report

4.1 Overall structure

The structure of the report should reflect the function. The questions that need to be answered are:

♦ Is there a specific aim?

♦ Is it just a presentation of facts?

♦ Does it need a demonstration of analysis used?

 All reports, whether short or long, formal or informal, need the basic structure of **beginning, middle and end.**

The **beginning** should determine:

♦ what the document is about;

♦ the relevance for the reader.

The **middle** should contain:

♦ the main analysis;

♦ the detailed argument supporting your conclusions, recommendations or proposed action.

The **end** should tell the reader:

♦ what will happen or what you want them to do;

♦ conclusions and recommendations.

4.2   *Checking the report*

After writing the report, the next step is the checking and preparation of the work for distribution.

The steps to follow when checking your report are:

(a)   Checking should not take place immediately after writing. If it is possible to come back to the report after a few days have lapsed, then checking is likely to be more effective.

(b)   Edit the report yourself before asking a colleague to look at it. Look at it with the following structure in mind.

   ♦   **Material**:

   Does the report contain all that should be included?

   Has unnecessary padding been taken out?

   ♦   **Language** (see later section on effective business communication):

   Are the words well chosen, precise and appropriate?

   Is their meaning clear?

   Is the report easy to read and understand?

   ♦   **Design**:

   Is it well planned?

   Are the sections in the right order?

   Are the paragraphs in logical sequence?

   Is it attractively set out?

(c)   Ask a **colleague to review it** and to identify:

   ♦   parts which are unclear;

   ♦   areas or points which you have missed;

   ♦   flaws in your argument.

(d)   Arrange a **meeting** to discuss your colleague's comments.

4.3   *Physical appearance*

As far as **physical appearance** is concerned, first impressions are very important and the report's physical appearance should be designed to create the desired impression.

4.4   *Page layout*

Good layout impresses readers. Make sure there is plenty of space between the various parts of the report and leave a good margin.

The different sections of the report usually begin on a **new page**, though the sub-sections of the main body of the report will generally follow on from one another.

For the typical text page of a report, a conventional layout is one that appears to fit the page as a picture in a frame. This layout fits the page **not covered by the binding of the report**. Thus the typist must allow an extra amount on the left margins of a left bound report and at the top of the pages in a top bound report.

4.5 Headings

Headings are the titles of the various **divisions of the report**. Usually, it helps if you make generous use of headings and sub-headings. Headings break text into manageable sections and help by increasing the 'white space' around the blocks of type, especially when the type is single spaced. They also act as signposts, pointing out what is to be found in each section.

Formal headings such as PROBLEM or EXPERIMENTAL or DISCUSSION are not as useful as informative headings that genuinely focus attention on the essence of the following paragraphs.

The importance of headings (sometimes called **captions**) is emphasised by type and position. There are four major positions of headings.

♦ Highest of these four in order of rank is the **centred heading**. This is on a line by itself and is centred between the right and left margins.

♦ Next in order is the **marginal heading**. Beginning on the left margin, this is also on a line by itself.

♦ The **box heading** is the next in the ranking. It begins on the left margin and is surrounded by a box of space formed by indenting the first few lines of the text.

♦ The fourth is the **run-in heading**. This simply runs into the first line of the text it covers and is distinguished from the text only by underscoring or using a bolder font or capitals.

4.6 The reader of the report

Whatever type of report you are preparing, it is vital to consider the **reader's interest** if you wish to convey your message. The audience you are trying to reach via the report will determine:

(1)   the language you use;

(2)   the length of the report;

(3)   the style of the report.

4.7 The language you use

The primary goal of report writers is to communicate the messages of their reports. Ideally they should communicate these messages as quickly, as easily and as precisely as language will permit.

To achieve a **more effective business writing style** there are a number of points to note.

4.8 Short words not long

Never use a long word where a short one will do.

Short words are easy to spell and understand and tend to communicate better than *long* words.

Can you think of short words for *perception, initiate* and *utilise*? It might be easier to use *view, start* or *use* instead of the longer words.

Readability studies show that a heavy proportion of long words tends to slow up the reading and makes understanding difficult.   Thus, wise report writers will use long words with caution.

The following contrasting **sentences** show the effect of long words on writing *clarity*.   Without question the simple versions communicate better.

A decision was predicated on the assumption that an abundance of monetary funds was forthcoming.	The decision was based on the belief that there would be more money.
They acceded to the proposition to terminate the business.	They agreed to end the business.
During the preceding year the company operated at a financial deficit.	Last year the company lost money.

Activity 1 *(The answer is in the final chapter of this book)*

Finding the right word

In the following sentences, replace the words printed in italics with more suitable words:

(a)   One statesman thought the treaty *derogative* to his country's honour.

(b)   The Frenchman regards the *observation* of the Sabbath from a different standpoint.

(c)   The town officials did their best to make the buses popular and *payable*.

(d)   Among the typists she raised such *dissent* that no pair of them remained on speaking terms.

(e)   Your best plan is to treat him as *contemptibly* as you can.

(f)   The body was so mangled that it could hardly be recognised as *humane*.

(g)   It seemed that the patient ought to *decease*.

(h)   The girl was *sick with nostalgia*.

(i)   By these remarks do you mean to *infer* that I know something about your savings?

(j)   I have photographed the children of that school now for thirty years without a *breakage*.

(k)   The island is famous for its *luxurious* vegetation.

(l)   The murderer was seen in the very *action* of firing his gun.

(m)   After the *invention* of chloroform surgical operations had a higher rate of success.

4.9   Active not passive

Prefer the active to the passive voice.

The active is more concise and forceful.

Compare the following.

The outstanding balance should be confirmed by the debtor (9 words).	The debtor should confirm the outstanding balance (7 words).
The stocktake was attended by the internal auditor (8 words).	The internal auditor attended the stocktake (6 words).
A receipt was issued by the wholesaler (7 words).	The wholesaler issued a receipt (5 words).

In each case the second sentence is said to be 'active', ie 'something or someone **does** something'.

The first sentence is 'passive' in comparison, ie. 'something or someone has something **done** to it '.

The passive takes more words to construct and, being clumsy, takes more effort to understand.

If you have a **passive sentence** try:

♦   changing 'X was done by Y' to 'Y did X';

♦   changing the verb eg. 'profits were reduced by' to 'profits fell by';

♦   changing the subject eg 'these recommendations can be implemented in two ways' to 'there are two ways to implement these recommendations'.

Having said this, it is only fair to point out that some formal reports do require the passive, third person.

4.10   Short sentences

Shortening sentences can improve clarity.

Compare the following.

The completion of the report should be before 28 March 20X7 (8 words and date).	The report should be completed by 28 March 20X7 (6 words and date).
There is no availability of computer expertise (7 words).	Computer expertise is not available (5 words).
The practicality of using value-weighted selection is in doubt (10 words).	Value-weighted selection may not be practical (7 words).

In each case the second sentence is easier to read and comprehend. In the first sentences the words such as practicality, availability and completion are warning signs that the sentence is not as simple as it might be.

4.11   Economy with words

Use words economically.

Our language is cluttered with phrases that are best replaced by shorter expressions. Although the shorter forms may save only a word or two here and there, the cumulative savings over a long piece of writing can be significant.

Some examples of long and short are:

Along the lines of	Like
For the purpose of	For
For the reason that	Because, since
In the near future	Soon
In short supply	Scarce
In accordance with	By
In several instances	Often
At this moment in time	Now
Prior to	Before
In very few cases	Seldom
A number of	Several
With regard to/in connection with	About
With the result that	So
With the minimum of delay	Quickly

4.12   Sentence length

Vary sentence length.

A sentence is a group of words that make complete sense. More than any other characteristic of a sentence, length is most clearly related to sentence difficulty. The longer a sentence is, the harder it is to understand.

When an excess of information is presented in a single package, the mind cannot grasp it all, at least on a single reading. Most current authorities agree that sentences aimed at the middle level of adult readers should average 16 to 18 words in length. For more advanced readers the average can be higher, and it must be lower for those of lower reading abilities. Of course, these figures do not mean that sentences of six or so words are taboo, nor do they mean that you should avoid long sentences of more than thirty words. It is the average that should be in keeping with the readability level of the reader.

4.13   Slang and foreign phrases

When we speak, we tailor our words to suit those to whom we speak; in writing, we address a wider audience and must use words which will be generally understood. It follows that certain words must be excluded from our written vocabulary since their meaning will not be clear to everyone. They fall into four classes.

Slang words are often vivid and effective in speech but should not be used in writing. Phrases such as 'get the push' and 'coming on heavy', should be replaced by standard English ones.

Words and phrases used only in certain districts are to be avoided for the same reason. They are excellent in speech, and often have more character than the corresponding words in standard English, yet, since they will not be generally understood, it is unwise to use them. The Scotsman may use 'wee' in speech, but he will use 'little' in written text.

Foreign words and phrases should be used as little as possible, unless they have already been absorbed into the language. Route, chef, chauffeur and matinee are French words that we could hardly do without, but you can usually avoid foreign phrases such as *inter alia, per annum, prima facie* and *carte blanche* by writing *among others, a year, at first sight* and *blank cheque* or *free hand*.

The UK and USA have been described as two countries divided by a common language. Not only does American spelling sometimes differ from ours but so do many expressions.

Activity 2 *(The answer is in the final chapter of this book)*

Not at all obvious

Look at the following extract from a written report:

> Ten newsagent shops in the Bristol area were selected to test the effectiveness of two different display stands in generating sales. For the purposes of the survey the shops were designated with the letters A–J.
>
> During the period 15 March to 20 March the total sales for the three items were recorded. Two different stands were used to display those items for sale. Five of the stands were the traditional sloping top 5 ft wide stand made of formica with perspex divisions while the other five were the metal revolving type, 2 ft in diameter. Shops A, C, D, G, I, used the traditional stand and shops B, E, F, H, J, used the revolving stand.
>
> Total sales of the items during the six day test period (Monday to Saturday inclusive) were as follows: Shops E, F, G, H showed sales of 435, 475, 286 and 575 cards and Shop I 275 with Shop J at 525.
>
> There is an obvious correlation between sales and type of display stand. This correlation is reflected in similar studies carried out in Manchester and Aberdeen.

This material is taken from a survey report. How well have you been able to assimilate the information? Was the correlation between the sales and the type of display stand quite as 'obvious' as the author suggests?

Required

(a)   Your immediate superior, Mrs Jenkins, has asked you to rewrite this report in the short report format illustrated in an earlier section, presenting the facts in a more understandable manner.

(b)   The second task is to write a memo to the author, Jo Bloggs, raising any further queries you may have about the survey report.

4.14   The length of the report

To answer the question as to how long a report should be, we need to refer back to its purpose, which is to convey information to particular readers or to answer a question.

Obviously there is no 'right' answer as to length. Verbal reports can be just a few words long; for example 'his condition is stable'. However, some academic works such as PhD theses may run to thousands of pages. The biggest indication of length should come in the specification of the request for the report, so the first general rule is:

♦   **Be sure you know what is expected of you before you begin.**

The **time allowed for the completion** of the report is another indication. If you telephone a hospital wanting a report on a sick relative you don't expect them to send you a dossier the following month. But if you are writing a project on alternative software for management information systems, your report is likely to cover at least a week's research and should reflect this.

The second general rule is only a clarification of the first and is to:

♦ **Confine yourself to the facts of the case you are reporting on.**

 These two general rules, as well as those in the previous section on the language that you use, should give an indication of the length of the report required.

4.15   The style of the report

Style is the fashion of writing that transforms some collection of facts into a readable document.

Since reports tend to be quite formal, they are usually written in a **formal language**.

The **level of formality** may be due to the type of report. Although some insurance reports on car accidents are portrayed on walls of insurance brokers as highly amusing, they are not intended to be, as most are very serious. On the other hand, if the organisation is not one that demands formality, an academic piece of work may seem out of place.

A lack of formal style in a written report by a junior member of staff when the report is being read by the managing director or chairman may be seen as being too familiar, unless informality is customary within that organisation.

 The essence of good style is to **avoid complex, stilted writing** and aim for a simple style that is the most clear and thus the most satisfactory.

5   Summary

When writing any type of report the following matters should be considered:

♦ Who is the report for? – this will affect the style and language used in the report.

♦ What is the time scale for production of the report? – as well as ensuring that the report is completed on time this will also affect the length of the report.

♦ The overall structure of the report – it must have a beginning, a middle and an end.

♦ The clarity of the communication – ensure that detailed calculations are set out in the appendix not in the main body of the report and that the language used makes the message of the report quite clear.

CHAPTER 3

Tables and diagrams

ASSESSMENT FOCUS

In many assessments you will be required to prepare a table to illustrate data that has been given in narrative form, or to be able to display given data in a diagrammatic form. This may be as part of the production of a report or as a separate exercise entirely.

This chapter covers the following Knowledge and Understanding and Performance Criteria of the AAT Syllabus.

> Reports are prepared in the appropriate form and presented to management within required timescales *(Performance Criteria element 7.1)*

> Tabulation of accounting and other quantitative information *(Knowledge and Understanding elements 7.1, 7.2)*

> Methods of presenting information: written reports; diagrammatic; tabular *(Knowledge and Understanding elements 7.1, 7.2)*

In order to cover these the following topics are included.

> Tabulation of narrative data

> Interpretation of data in tabular form

> Pictograms

> Pie charts

> Simple bar charts

> Component bar charts

> Percentage component bar charts

> Compound bar charts

> The general rules to follow when drawing diagrams

1 Tables

1.1 Introduction

Most methods of data collection will result in **large amounts of data** being available. This is the case when an organisation's own internal sources are used or when the data collection is by either a survey or abstraction from secondary sources. These large amounts of data will need to be examined to obtain relevant information. This means we must discard any irrelevant details, usually leaving us with a number of categories and sub-categories from which we wish to obtain some overall impression. The data remaining from the elimination of irrelevant details can be summarised using either **narrative** or **tables**.

A **major drawback of the narrative approach** is that the information required is not clearly presented and only a limited amount of data can be presented. A properly constructed tabular presentation, however, gives the required information immediately and clearly.

1.2   Example

A major bank is interested in the types of account held by its customers. The information below has recently been collected:

A sample of 5,000 accounts was taken, each account belonging to a different customer. 729 accounts were held by customers aged under 25 of whom 522 held current accounts, the remainder holding ordinary deposit accounts. 1,383 of the accounts were held by customers aged between 25 and 44, 1,020 being current accounts, 271 were ordinary deposit accounts and the remainder were high-interest deposit accounts. There were 1,621 accounts belonging to customers aged between 45 and 59, of these 61% were current accounts, 29% were ordinary deposit accounts and 10% high interest deposit accounts. Of customers aged 60 and over, 628 held current accounts, 410 held ordinary deposit accounts and the remainder held high interest deposit accounts.

Summarise the information contained in this narrative into a single table.

1.3   Solution

(a)   **A simple one-way table**

A major point of interest in the given data is obviously the age breakdown of account holders. Working through the narrative, this could be presented as follows:

under 25	729
25–44	1,383
45–59	1,621
60 and over	1,267

The figure for the 60 and over group is given by 5,000 – (729 + 1,383 + 1,621) since there are a total of 5,000 accounts each held by different customers.

(b)   **Title and headings**

The table in (a) gives us a clear breakdown of the ages of the customers but leaves the reader to guess what the columns mean. Clearly the left-hand column is age but it is better to label both columns clearly and to tell the reader what the subject of the table is. Also it is useful to show relevant totals, ie. in this case the total number of accounts.

An improvement on the table given in (a) is thus as follows:

Ages of customers

Age	Number of customers
under 25	729
25–44	1,383
45–59	1,621
60 and over	1,267
	___
Total	5,000
	___

(c)   **Another one-way table**

Another major point of interest in the data is the number of accounts held of each type. A table of this information is more difficult to extract from the narrative and some steps of working may be helpful.

(1)   There are three types of account: current accounts, ordinary deposit accounts and high interest deposit accounts.

(2)   Current accounts:

522 (age under 25);

1,020 (aged 25–44);

989 (aged 45–59; 61% of 1,621 accounts = 0.61 × 1,621 = 988.81 or 989 accounts by rounding to nearest whole number of accounts);

628 (aged 60 and over).

(3)   Ordinary deposit accounts:

207 (aged under 25; ie. 729 minus the number of current accounts = 729 – 522);

271 (aged 25–44);

470 (aged 45–59; 29% of 1,621 accounts = 0.29 × 1,621 = 470);

410 (aged 60 and over).

(4)   High interest deposit account:

0 (aged under 25; we must assume this since no other detail is given);

92 (aged 25–44; 1,383 minus the number of current and ordinary deposit accounts = 1,383 – (1,020 + 271) = 1,383 – 1,291);

162 (aged 45 – 59; 10% of 1,621 accounts = 0.10 × 1,621 = 162.1 or 162);

229 (aged 60 and over; total aged 60 and over minus number of current and ordinary deposit accounts = 1,267 (from (a)) – (628 + 410) = 229).

Summing the number of accounts in (2) to (4) gives the required table.

Number of different accounts held

Type of account	Number of customers
Current	3,159
Ordinary deposit	1,358
High interest deposit	483
Total	5,000

(d)   **A two-way table**

Our objective at the start of this example was to construct a single table to summarise all the information contained in the narrative. Having carried out the simple calculations in (c) above, this is now easily done by employing a two-way table (sometimes called a cross-tabulation). In this example the two 'variables' are obviously age of customers and type of account held. These become the headings for the following required two-way table.

Ages and types of account held by sample of 5,000 customers

	Age				
Type of account	*under 25*	*25–44*	*45–59*	*60 and over*	*Total*
Current	522	1,020	989	628	3,159
Ordinary deposit	207	271	470	410	1,358
High interest deposit	0	92	162	229	483
Total	729	1,383	1,621	1,267	5,000

1.4 Guidelines for constructing tables

There are no set rules for constructing tables since tables often vary markedly in content and format. The following **guidelines** should however be adhered to:

♦ Always give the table a **title** and suitable **headings**.

♦ If the data contains a number of categories or sub-categories, use a **two-way table**.

♦ Give column and row **sub-totals** where appropriate.

♦ If the draft table contains too much detail, it will fail in its objective of summarising the data. **Further simplified tables** should then be constructed, each dealing with different aspects of the data.

♦ It is important to state the **source of the data**. This may be included in the title or given beneath the table.

♦ The **units in the table** should be 'manageable'. This can be accomplished by, for example, dividing particular column entries by 1,000 and including this fact in the column heading.

♦ It is sometimes useful to show **percentages** in the table in addition to the actual figures.

In analysing large amounts of data, tables similar to those already considered prove very useful. They simplify a mass of narrative into columns and rows of figures which are much easier to understand.

1.5 Example

Smith plc manufactures bed linen. In 20X2 its total sales were £126,000 and these sales increased by £28,000 in 20X3 and then again by £41,000 in 20X4. In comparison Brown plc, one of Smith's competitors, had total sales of £206,000 in 20X2 and their sales reduced by 10% each year in 20X3 and 20X4. Present this information in tabular form.

1.6 Solution

Step 1 It is useful in any problem where construction of a table is required to first write down the headings in the table. In this example this is easy:

Year   *Sales of Smith plc*   *Sales of Brown plc*

Step 2 The next stage in problems of this kind is to work out the individual entries in the table:

Smith plc:	20X2	£126,000
	20X3	£126,000 + £28,000 = £154,000
	20X4	£154,000 + £41,000 = £195,000
Brown plc:	20X2	£206,000
	20X3	£206,000 – (0.1 × £206,000) = £206,000 – £20,600 = £185,400
	20X4	£185,400 – (0.1 × £185,400) = £185,400 – £18,540 = £166,860

Step 3 The draft table is now easily formed:

Year	*Sales of Smith plc* £	*Sales of Brown plc* £
20X2	126,000	206,000
20X3	154,000	185,400
20X4	195,000	166,860

Step 4 Since the units are all of the same order of magnitude, we can make the units more manageable by dividing by 1,000 although it might be acceptable to round Brown's figures to the nearest £'000. Also a title should be added to the table. The final table might thus have the form:

Sales of Smith plc and Brown plc for 20X2 – X4

Year	*Sales of Smith plc* £000	*Sales of Brown plc* £000
20X2	126	206
20X3	154	185
20X4	195	167

When planning your table try to minimise the number of columns across the page. Therefore in this example it is better to have the sales of Smith plc and Brown plc as the columns rather than to have a column for each year.

Activity 1 *(The answer is in the final chapter of this book)*

Bunny and Hutch

The total number of employees of Bunny and Hutch Ltd on 31 December 20X4 was 3,984, of which 2,124 were men. During 20X4, 221 men had been engaged and 185 resigned. The corresponding figures for women were 97 and 108 respectively. Because of the different types of work done, the average wage rate paid to male employees in 20X4 was £121.32 and to female employees £87.93. The company worked for 50 weeks in 20X4. Tabulate this data, including in your table an estimate of the total wage bill.

1.7   Analysis of tables

In some instances instead of drawing up a table you may be required to analyse or interpret the information in a table.

1.8   Example

The table below shows figures of employees in different types of employment for the years 20X2 to 20Y3. Interpret this data by commenting on the trend in employment in motor vehicle manufacturing and comparing it to what happened in 'manufacturing' and 'all industries and services'.

Total employees in employment

Year	Motor vehicle manufacturing '000	Manufacturing '000	All industries and services '000
20X2	490	7,779	22,121
20X3	510	7,830	22,663
20X4	497	7,873	22,790
20X5	457	7,524	22,710
20X6	448	7,281	22,543
20X7	464	7,328	22,619
20X8	471	7,290	22,777
20X9	459	7,258	23,158
20Y0	412	6,940	22,972
20Y1	355	6,221	21,871
20Y2	318	5,912	21,473
20Y3	306	5,641	21,210

Source: *Employment Gazette*

1.9   Solution

Questions of this type are a little vague in what is required. For each of the three columns of data on employment we could, for example, comment on every year to year change, eg. employment in motor vehicle manufacturing increased by 20,000 from 20X2 to 20X3, fell by 13,000 from 20X3 to 20X4, etc. This is clearly a long-winded way of describing the trend in employment and should be avoided.

What is required is some comment on the general changes in employment, without too much detail. For all questions of this type this is best achieved by picking out the 'peaks' and 'troughs' in the data and also by commenting on the overall change in the data between the beginning of the period and the end. In this example, suitable comments might be as follows.

♦   The total number of employees in motor vehicle manufacturing has shown a decreasing trend over the period. It rose to a peak in 20X3, gradually fell until 20X6, increased slightly until 20X8 and then fell dramatically until 20Y3 when it was over 37% down on the 20X2 figure.

♦   The total number of employees in manufacturing industries also fell, on average, over the period. It rose slowly between 20X2 and 20X4 but then fell sharply until 20X6, when after a small increase in 20X7, it fell rapidly until 20Y3. Overall between 20X2 and 20Y3 there was a 27.5% fall in employment in manufacturing industries.

◆ The total number of employees in all industries and services showed far less fluctuation than the previous two sets of figure. The total rose between 20X2 and 20X4, fell back between 20X4 and 20X6, rose again to peak in 20X9 and then fell fairly sharply until 20Y3 when it was just over 4% below the 20X2 figure.

Workings

Percentage changes in employment between 20X2 and 20Y3:

motor vehicle manufacturing $= \dfrac{490 - 306}{490} \times 100\% \quad = 37.55\%$ fall

manufacturing $= \dfrac{7{,}779 - 5{,}641}{7{,}779} \times 100\% \quad = 27.48\%$ fall

all industries and services $= \dfrac{22{,}121 - 21{,}210}{22{,}121} \times 100\% \quad = 4.12\%$ fall

It is also useful in questions of this type to give some overall comment about what appears to be happening (as indicated by the data).

In this example, there has obviously been a large movement of employees out of motor vehicle manufacturing between 20X2 and 20Y3. On the limited evidence available, this movement of employees does not seem to have been into other manufacturing industries since there has also been a 27.5% fall in employment in this area.

Activity 2 *(The answer is in the final chapter of this book)*

Motor policies

The following table gives details of the motor insurance policies of an insurance company in 20X3.

Region	Number of claims	Number of policies held
North	1,330	16,223
Midlands	1,384	18,210
South	1,377	22,581
East Anglia	234	9,363
London	1,401	32,580
Wales	180	10,005
Scotland	118	7,388
Northern Ireland	659	6,276

Provide a brief interpretation of the information contained in this table.

2 Diagrams

2.1 Introduction

Diagrams are a further way in which information can be presented in a readily understandable way. There are a variety of different types of diagrams that can be used to illustrate data and the choice of the most appropriate type will depend upon:

- the type of data

- the amount of data

- the factors that you wish to emphasise

2.2 Pictograms

A pictogram is a simple diagram which uses pictures to represent numbers.

2.3 Example

The number of letters received by five mail order firms in a year are given below:

Firm	Annual number of letters
Great Galaxy	3,475,000
Commonwealth	8,022,000
Largeforests	5,308,000
Ells	4,427,000
Berties	6,381,000

2.4 Solution

We could use a picture of a letter to represent a number of actual letters. In this case if we use a picture of a letter to represent 1,000,000 letters received, we obtain the pictogram below.

Annual number of letters

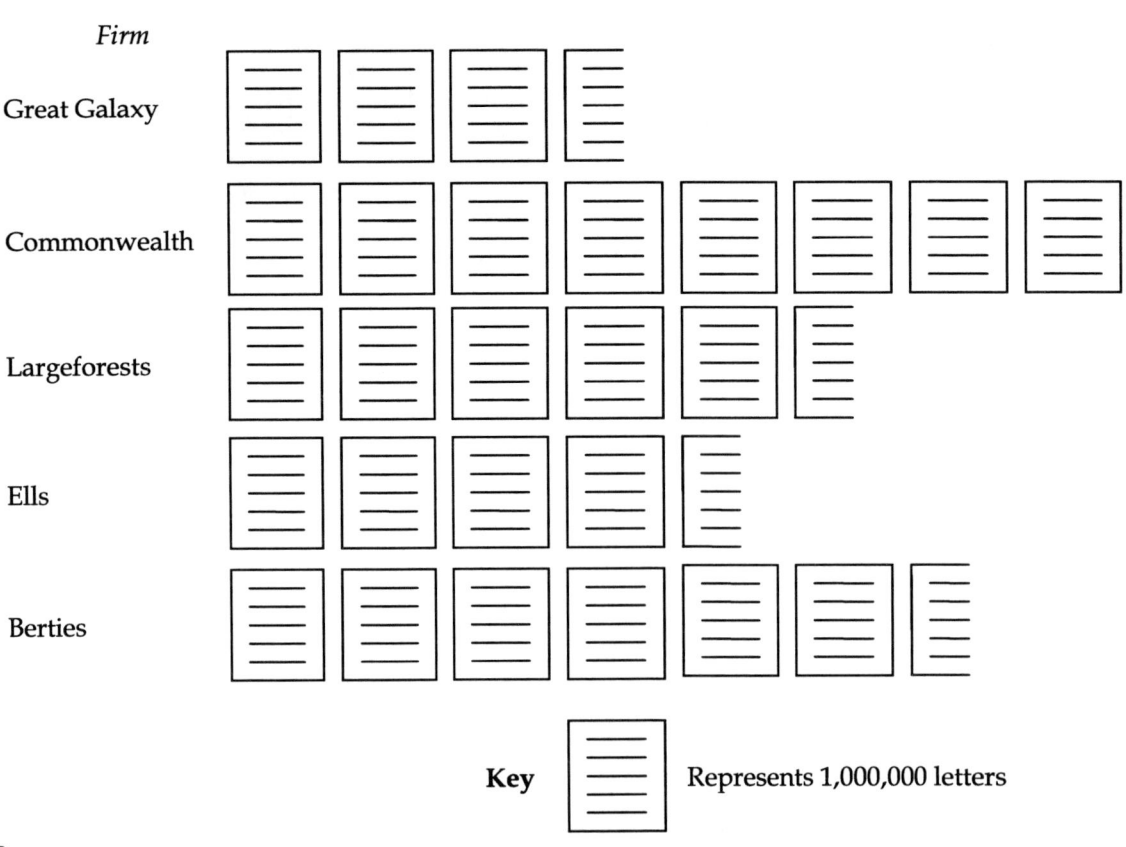

Always remember to include the **key** on your diagram.

As can be seen fractions in the pictogram are difficult to show accurately, but that is not the purpose of these diagrams. They are to give us a **quick, rough idea of relative size** and as such are fairly successful.

An alternative approach sometimes adopted is to magnify the picture so that its size represents the figure being illustrated as shown below.

Great Galaxy

Commonwealth

Largeforests

Ells

Berties

Key Represents 1,000,000 letters

2.5   Example

Draw an appropriate pictogram for the following beer sales figures.

Brewery	*Quarterly sales figure*
	(£)
Soprano	542,000
Blackdough	397,000
Empties	56,000
Browns	315,000

2.6   Solution

(Probably the easiest picture to use is a glass of beer.)

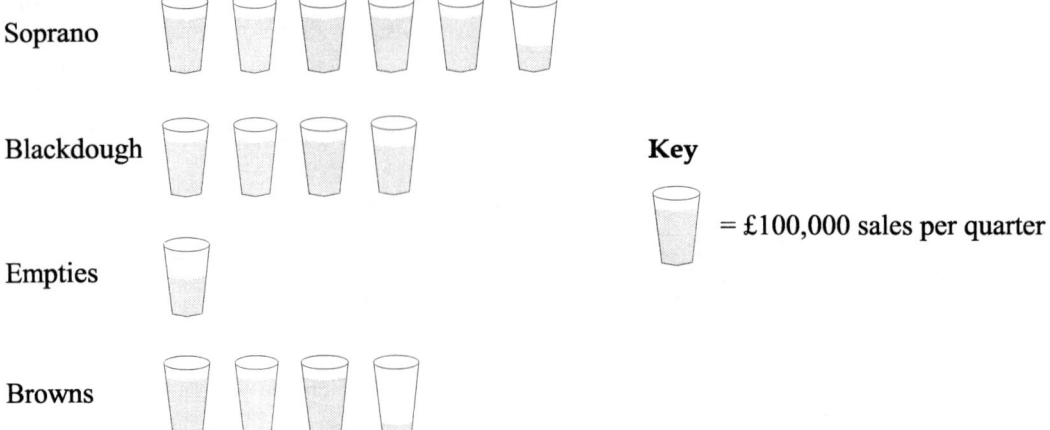

2.7 Pie charts

A **pie chart** consists of a circle split into segments. The circle represents a total and the segments represent the parts which go to make up the total. The 360° of the circle is divided in proportion to the figures making the total.

2.8 Example

Suppose a family's income in 20X5 is £1,000 per month, and their expenditure splits down as follows.

	Amount	Proportion	Angle
	£	%	(degrees)
Mortgage and insurance	300	30	108
Electricity and gas	50	5	18
Food and drink	200	20	72
Clothes	40	4	14
Car and petrol	150	15	54
Telephone	10	1	4
Savings	70	7	25
Fares	60	6	22
Miscellaneous	120	12	43
	1,000	100	360

2.9 Solution

The resulting pie chart would look like this:

Key

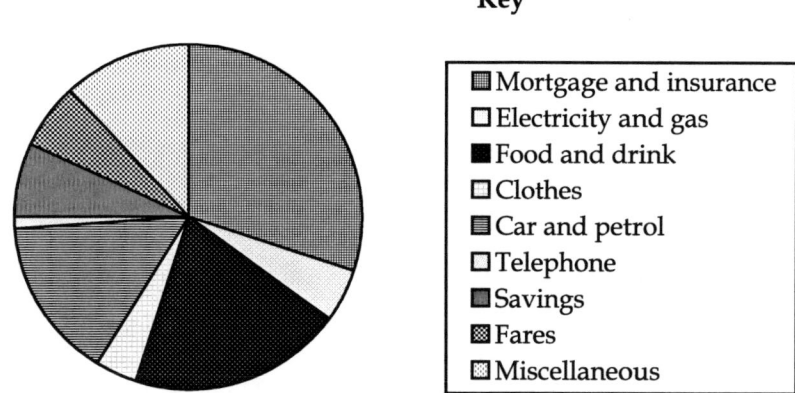

■ Mortgage and insurance
□ Electricity and gas
■ Food and drink
□ Clothes
▦ Car and petrol
□ Telephone
▨ Savings
▨ Fares
▨ Miscellaneous

 You can either use the names in the segments or represent each category by a different colour or shading, provided a key is given.

 Again, we do not obtain a precise idea of expenditure on certain items or services, just an idea of their **relative proportions**.

2.10   Example

Draw a pie chart for the following data.

Breakdown of grocery market share

Food Inc	29%
Grub plc	22%
Cookers	15%
Troughers	13%
Others	21%

2.11   Solution

Number of degrees:

	Percentage	Angle°	
Food Inc	29%	$360 \times 0.29 =$	104
Grub plc	22%	$360 \times 0.22 =$	79
Cookers	15%	$360 \times 0.15 =$	54
Troughers	13%	$360 \times 0.13 =$	47
Others	21%	$360 \times 0.21 =$	76
	100		360

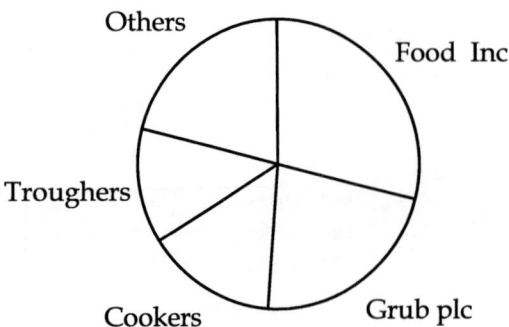

Activity 3 *(The answer is in the final chapter of this book)*

WMSC (AAT CA D94 – amended)

The administration manager of WMSC, a charter shipping organisation, receives regular information on the analysis of the general expenses in the form of pie charts. He is having some difficulty in understanding the charts and, to make matters worse, when last month's charts were sent out, the 'key' was not completed.

Required

(a)   Use the figures provided to complete the key to the pie charts by identifying which segment (labelled A to E) represents which expense. If you think A = Depreciation then write A opposite Depreciation in the letter column.

	November 20X6 £'000	November 20X5 £'000
Wages and salaries	69	53
Building occupation costs	46	52
Agents' commission	58	42
General administration expenses	23	31
Depreciation	34	32
	230	210

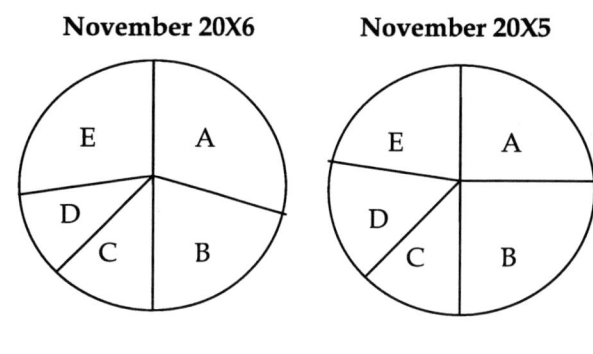

Key	Letter
Wages & salaries	. . . . . .
Building occupation	. . . . . .
Agents' commission	. . . . . .
General admin. expenses	. . . . . .
Depreciation	. . . . . .

(b)   Write a short report to the administration manager:

   (i)   explaining the main points that are revealed by a comparison of the pie charts;

   (ii)   suggesting an explanation for the changes in the agents' commission and the general administration expenses.

3   Bar charts

3.1   Introduction

One popular method of illustrating data in order to compare it or show its changes over time is to show it in the form of a bar chart. There are a number of different types of bar chart to consider:

♦   a simple bar chart

♦   a component bar chart

♦   a percentage component bar chart

♦   a compound bar chart

We shall look at each type in turn.

3.2   Simple bar charts

In a **simple bar chart** the figures we wish to compare are represented by bars. These can either be drawn vertically or horizontally. The height or length of a bar is proportional to the size of the figure being illustrated.

3.3   Example

The production figures of different car companies are given:

Firm	Number of cars produced
Ausota	180,000
Vauxsun	145,000
Moruar	165,000
Trihall	160,000
Fortin	170,000

3.4   Solution

A vertical bar chart can be prepared as follows:

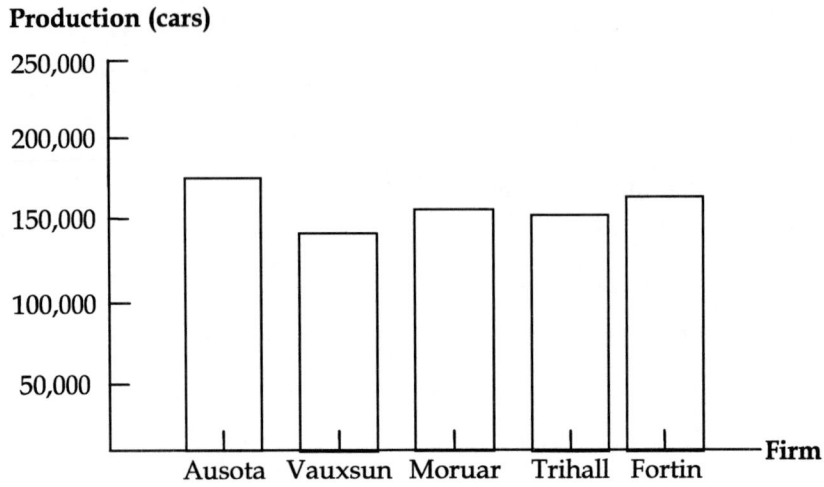

Alternatively the data could be shown in a horizontal bar chart.

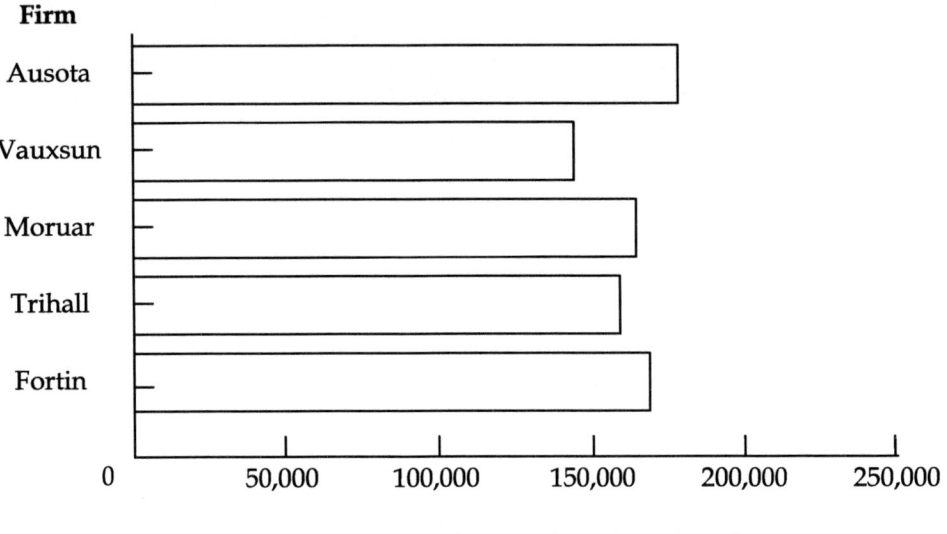

 Vertical bar charts are much more commonly used than horizontal ones, therefore in an assessment produce the vertical version unless specifically asked for a horizontal one.

 We can put the **appropriate identification** either in the bar itself, immediately adjacent to the bar, or use a key for shadings or colours. When drawing these charts it is very important to start the scale from zero. A misleading picture may be shown otherwise.

3.5   Example

Draw a simple bar chart of the following figures for the number of branches of certain chain stores:

Chain store	Branches
AZX	360
Blazes	245
D & L	185
Cottonvalue	290
Allsorts	410

3.6   Solution

Bar chart showing the number of branches

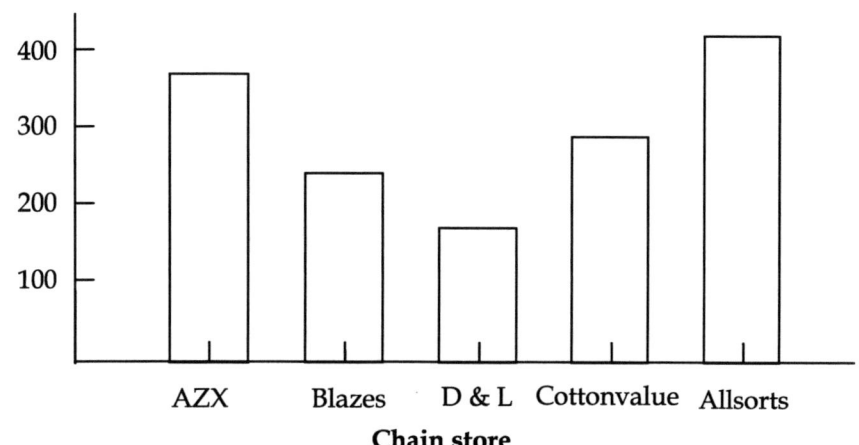

 Always ensure that the bar chart has a title and that both axes are labelled to make it clear what the bar chart is illustrating.

3.7   Component bar charts

When we draw bar charts the totals we wish to illustrate can often be broken down into **sub-divisions or components.** These sub-divisions can be clearly illustrated using a component bar chart.

3.8   Example

Wine consumption by type for a year is shown below.

	Consumption figures (10,000 litres)			
	Red	White	Rosé	Total
20X2	59.3	46.5	14.2	120.0
20X3	63.6	47.0	14.4	125.0
20X4	72.3	48.2	14.5	135.0

3.9   Solution

We start by drawing a **simple bar chart** of the total figures. The columns or bars are then **split up into the component parts**.

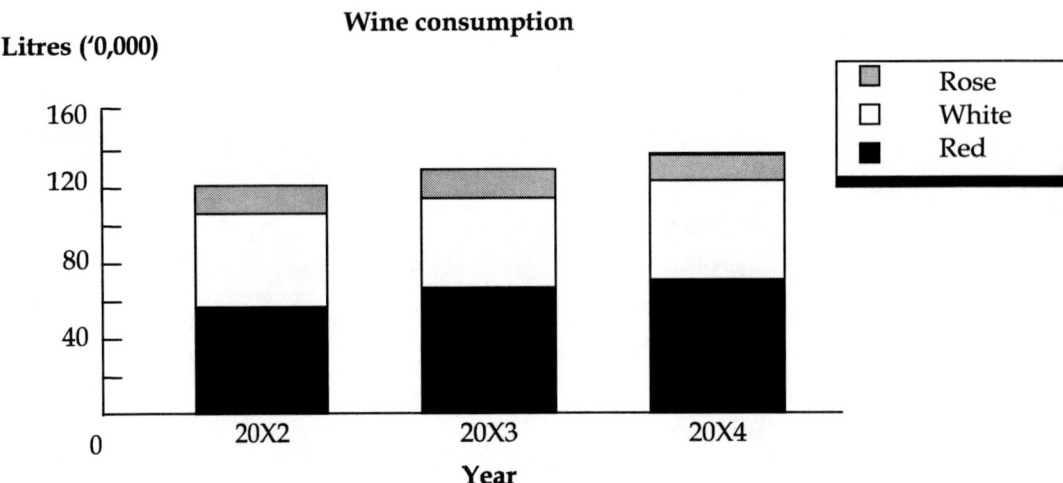

 You must have a key showing what each component relates to otherwise the chart will not provide any useful information.

3.10   Example

A shoe firm has three factories. The output of pairs of shoes by factory is:

	20X1	20X2	20X3	20X4
Leicester	350,000	300,000	550,000	400,000
Northampton	200,000	300,000	400,000	500,000
Nottingham	200,000	300,000	300,000	400,000

Draw a suitable diagram to illustrate this information.

3.11   Solution

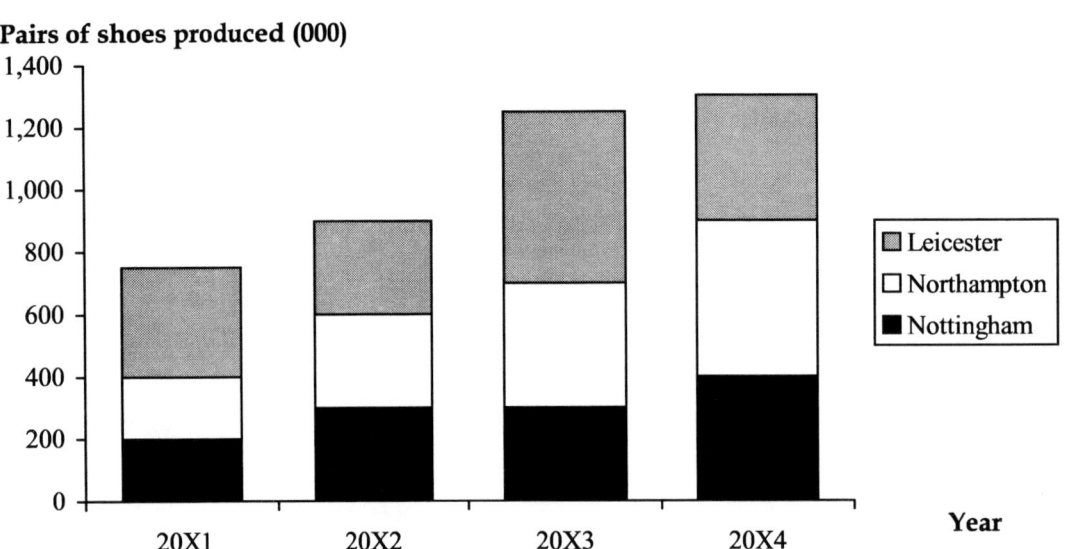

Notice that you **need to calculate cumulative totals** in order to plot these diagrams by hand, eg the total for Nottingham plus Northampton then the total for all three factories.

Component bar charts are useful for illustrating both how total figures have been changed as well as their component elements.

3.12   Percentage component bar chart

If we wish to know what **proportion** of a total each component represents, we can use a **percentage component bar chart** in place of a pie chart. All the columns of the bar chart are the same height or length representing 100%. These are then divided in the appropriate proportions.

3.13   Example

Using the wine consumption figures again, the proportions for each type of wine consumption are calculated as:

	Red	*White*	*Rose*
20X2	$\dfrac{59.3}{120.0} \times 100 = 49.4\%$	$\dfrac{46.5}{120.0} \times 100 = 38.8\%$	$\dfrac{14.2}{120.0} \times 100 = 11.8\%$
20X3	$\dfrac{63.6}{125.0} \times 100 = 50.9\%$	$\dfrac{47.0}{125.0} \times 100 = 37.6\%$	$\dfrac{14.4}{125.0} \times 100 = 11.5\%$
20X4	$\dfrac{72.3}{135.0} \times 100 = 53.6\%$	$\dfrac{48.2}{135.0} \times 100 = 35.7\%$	$\dfrac{14.5}{135.0} \times 100 = 10.7\%$

Draw a percentage component bar chart.

3.14   Solution

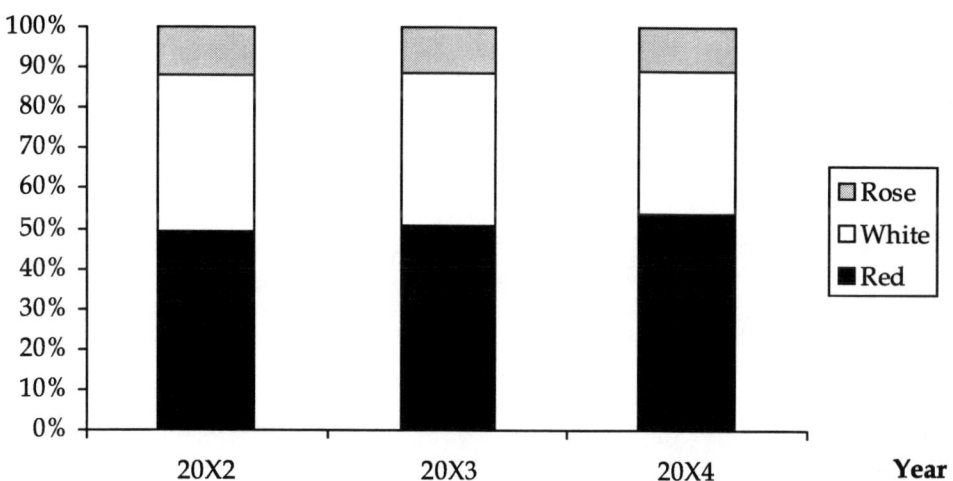

Wine consumption

3.15 Example

The shoe production figures are given again below.

	20X1	20X2	20X3	20X4
Leicester	350,000	300,000	550,000	400,000
Northampton	200,000	300,000	400,000	500,000
Nottingham	200,000	300,000	300,000	400,000

Draw a percentage component bar chart for the shoe production data.

3.16 Solution

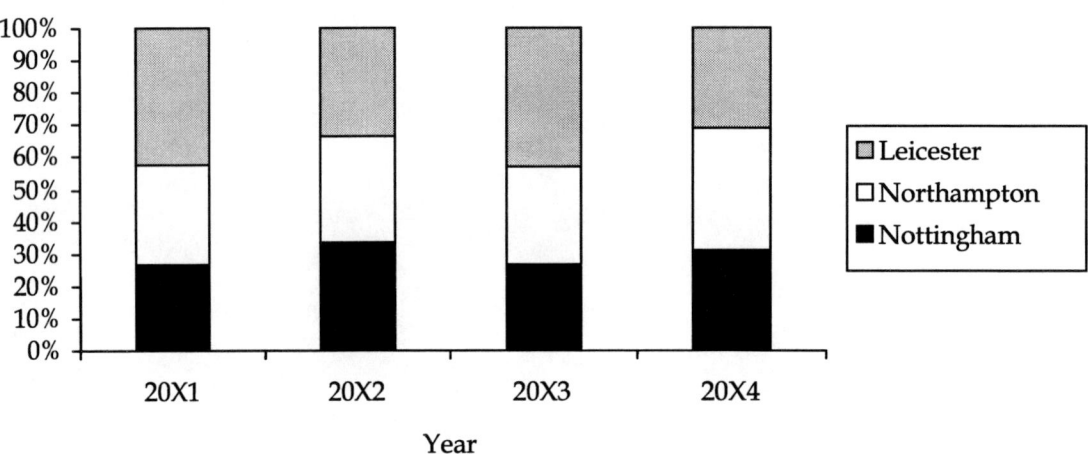

The proportions are worked out using the totals for each year, giving:

	Leicester	*Northampton*	*Nottingham*
20X1	$\frac{350,000}{750,000} \times 100 = 46.6\%$	$\frac{200,000}{750,000} \times 100 = 26.7\%$	$\frac{200,000}{750,000} \times 100 = 26.7\%$
20X2	$\frac{300,000}{900,000} \times 100 = 33.3\%$	$\frac{300,000}{900,000} \times 100 = 33.3\%$	$\frac{300,000}{900,000} \times 100 = 33.3\%$
20X3	$\frac{550,000}{1,250,000} \times 100 = 44.0\%$	$\frac{400,000}{1,250,000} \times 100 = 32.0\%$	$\frac{300,000}{1,250,000} \times 100 = 24.0\%$
20X4	$\frac{400,000}{1,300,000} \times 100 = 30.8\%$	$\frac{500,000}{1,300,000} \times 100 = 38.4\%$	$\frac{400,000}{1,300,000} \times 100 = 30.8\%$

Again the cumulative percentages must be calculated eg Nottingham plus Northampton then all three factories.

Percentage component bar charts do not illustrate how total figures have changed but they do clearly show how the elements of the total have changed.

Activity 4 (The answer is in the final chapter of this book)

Engineering assets

The accounts of an engineering company contain data on the value of its assets over the last five years as follows:

Asset	20X1 £'000	20X2 £'000	20X3 £'000	20X4 £'000	20X5 £'000
Property	59	59	65	70	74
Plant and machinery	176	179	195	210	200
Stock and work in progress	409	409	448	516	479
Debtors	330	313	384	374	479
Cash	7	60	29	74	74

Required

(a)   Compare the values of the assets by constructing a component bar chart and a percentage component bar chart.

(b)   Calculate the percentage increase in total value of assets over the five-year period.

(c)   Comment on the movements in the assets over the five-year period in a short memorandum report to the manager, Mr Joseph.

3.15   Compound bar charts

Our concern may not be with proportional comparisons but rather with **comparisons of the component figures themselves.** If this is the case we can use a **compound bar chart** where there is a bar for each component.

3.16   Example

The wine data is given again below.

Consumption figures

(10,000 litres)

	Red	White	Rosé	Total
20X2	59.3	46.5	14.2	120.0
20X3	63.6	47.0	14.4	125.0
20X4	72.3	48.2	14.5	135.0

3.17   Solution

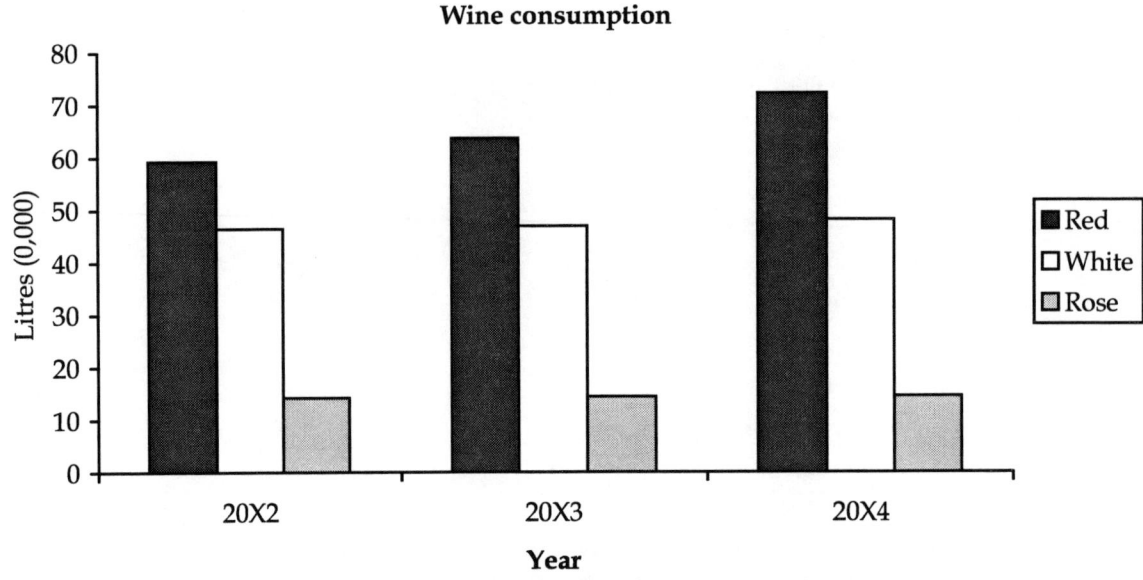

 This type of chart allows us to follow **trends of each individual component** as well as make comparisons between the components. It does not, however, give any direct indication of total consumption.

3.18   Example

The shoe production data is given again.

	20X1	20X2	20X3	20X4
Leicester	350,000	300,000	550,000	400,000
Northampton	200,000	300,000	400,000	500,000
Nottingham	200,000	300,000	300,000	400,000

Draw a compound bar chart for the shoe production data.

3.19   Solution

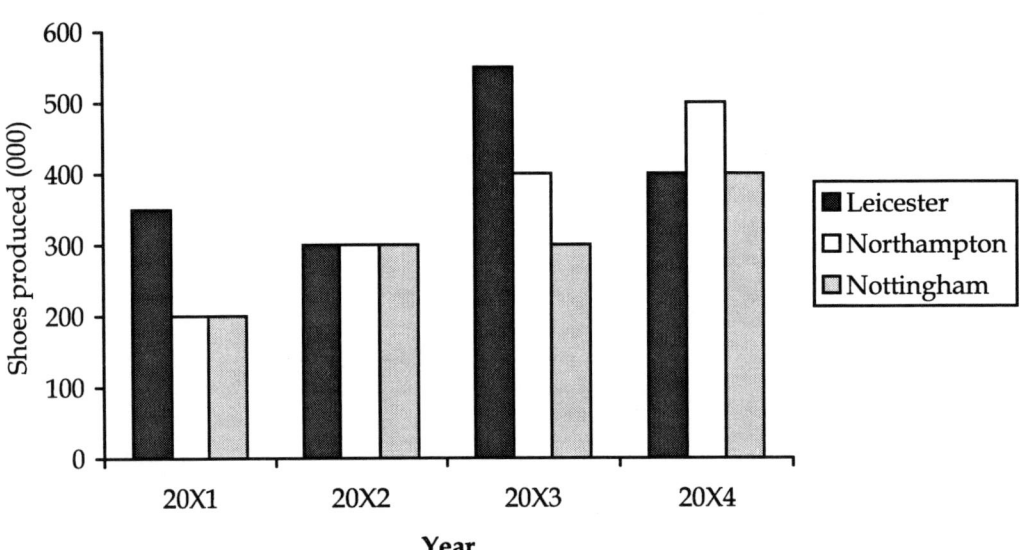

Activity 5 *(The answer is in the final chapter of this book)*

Energy consumption

The table below shows the total UK inland energy consumption, measured in millions of tonnes of coal equivalent, for coal, petroleum and natural gas in the years 20X1 and 20X9.

Energy type	20X1	20X9
Coal	139.3	129.6
Petroleum	151.2	139.0
Natural gas	28.8	71.3

Illustrate this data pictorially using (a) a component bar chart and (b) a compound bar chart. Discuss the benefits in using each method.

4 Rules for drawing charts and diagrams

4.1 Rules to follow

When drawing diagrams there are several points to consider:

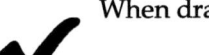

(a)   Try to make the diagrams **neat** and **uncluttered**. Use a **ruler**.

(b)   If **graph paper** is available, use it.

(c)   The diagram should have a **title**.

(d)   The **variables and scales** should be shown on each **axis**.

(e)   Set the scale so that you use **as much of the paper as you can** for the diagram; this will keep the diagram neater and assist accuracy.

(f)   Units must be indicated on **both axes**.

(g)   Where diagrams are combined or superimposed ensure that each is **recognisable separately** and suitably labelled.

(h)   **Too much detail** on a diagram makes it confusing rather than enlightening.

(i)   Remember the **key** where appropriate.

(j)   Remember to **start scales at** *zero* **on bar charts**.

(k)   Remember that **component and compound bar charts** become less and less effective the more sub-divisions you use. It is often worth considering **a pie chart as an alternative**.

4.2 Example

In the financial year 20X3/X4 Sheffield City Council had the following major items of expenditure:

	£m
Education	175
Housing	84
Family and community services	41
Policy and general purposes	17
Recreation and amenities	11
Environmental health and cleansing	11
Corporate estate	8

Illustrate this information.

4.3 Solution

Adding the figures up, the total expenditure was £347m. Given the number of categories, the clearest form for our illustration will be a pie chart. We must now work out the *proportions* of each category of expenditure and its angle.

	%	Angle
Education	$\dfrac{175}{347} \times 100 = 51$	$\dfrac{51}{100} \times 360 = 184$
Housing	$\dfrac{84}{347} \times 100 = 24$	$\dfrac{24}{100} \times 360 = 86$
Family & community services	$\dfrac{41}{347} \times 100 = 12$	$\dfrac{12}{100} \times 360 = 43$
Policy & general purposes	$\dfrac{17}{347} \times 100 = 5$	$\dfrac{5}{100} \times 360 = 18$
Recreation & amenities	$\dfrac{11}{347} \times 100 = 3$	$\dfrac{3}{100} \times 360 = 11$
Env. health & cleansing	$\dfrac{11}{347} \times 100 = 3$	$\dfrac{3}{100} \times 360 = 11$
Corporate estate	$\dfrac{8}{347} \times 100 = 2$	$\dfrac{2}{100} \times 360 = 7$
	100	360

The pie chart for the Sheffield City Council items of major expenditure is as follows.

Major expenditure of Sheffield City Council 20X3/X4

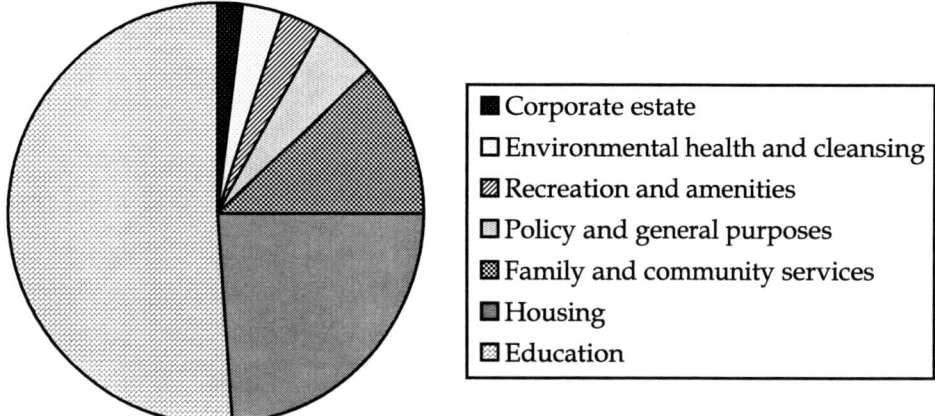

Corporate estate
Environmental health and cleansing
Recreation and amenities
Policy and general purposes
Family and community services
Housing
Education

Note: This example is a good illustration of the problem of rounding errors. The % column originally added up to 99% (not 100%) and the angle column to 356° (not 360°), making the illustration only approximate. Education's percentage (50.43%) was rounded up to 51%. The angles were recalculated with these percentages and the problem disappeared.

4.4   Comment on diagrams

In some instances you may be required to comment upon or analyse the data shown in a diagram.

4.5   Example

A computer company has three factories, located in Nottingham, Leicester and Derby. The production records of each factory are as follows.

	Number of computers produced (hundreds)		
Factory	20X2	20X3	20X4
Nottingham	3	5	14
Leicester	11	14	27
Derby	18	26	55
Total	32	45	96

Compare and contrast the production at the three factories using the component and percentage component bar charts given below (You do not need to calculate the percentages.)

Component bar chart

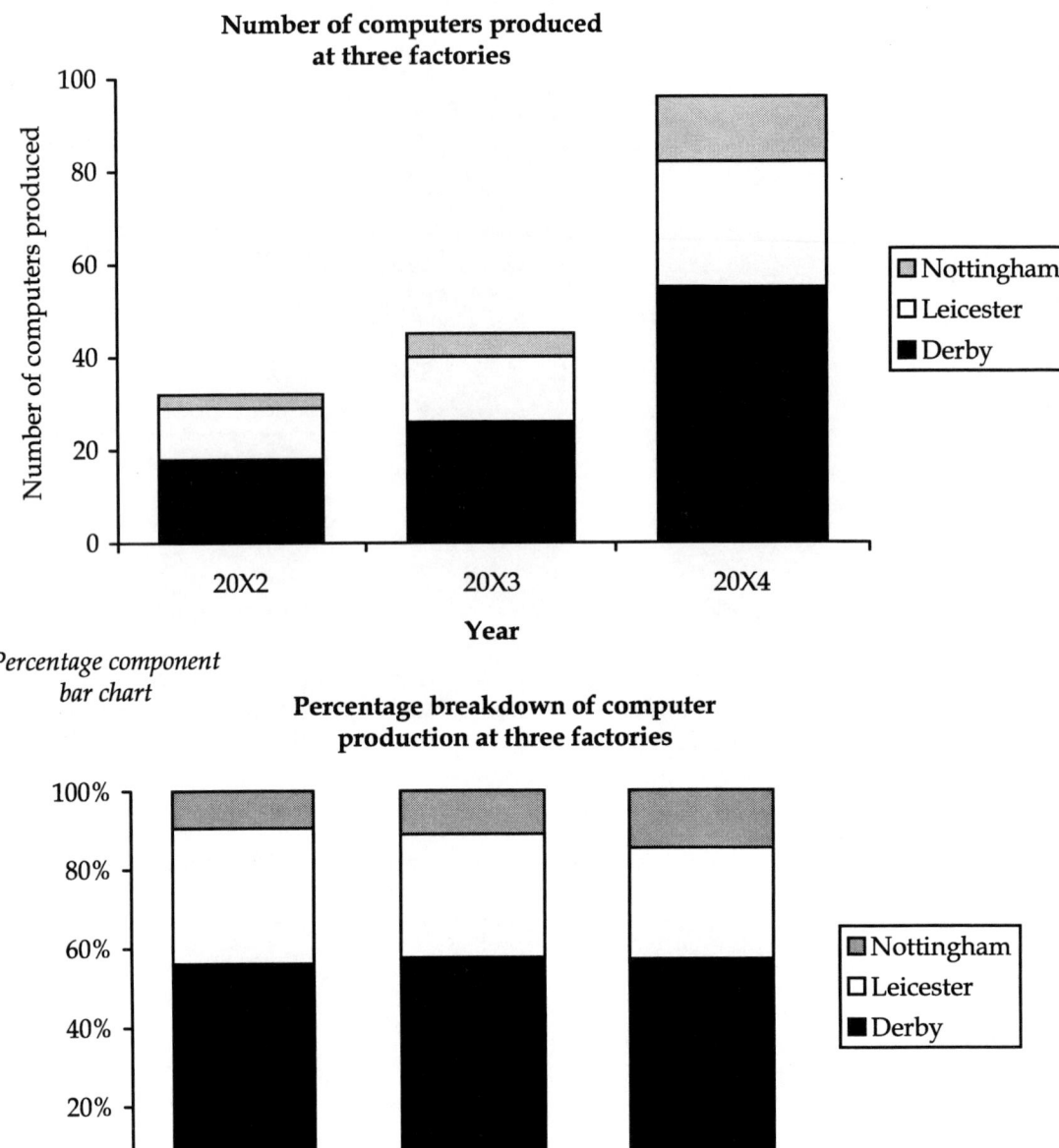

Percentage component bar chart

4.6 Solution

The component bar chart shows that:

♦ total production has increased year by year;

♦ production at the three factories has increased year by year;

♦ production was greatest at Derby, second highest at Leicester and smallest at Nottingham in each of the three years.

The percentage component bar chart shows that Nottingham has been producing an increasing proportion of total production, whilst Leicester's proportionate production has declined. Derby's proportionate production stayed about the same for each of the three years.

4.7   Example

The following chart shows the average annual salaries of employees of BS Ltd for 20X1 to 20X3. List the major points of information shown by this diagram, and comment on its preparation.

Average annual salaries of employees of BS Ltd

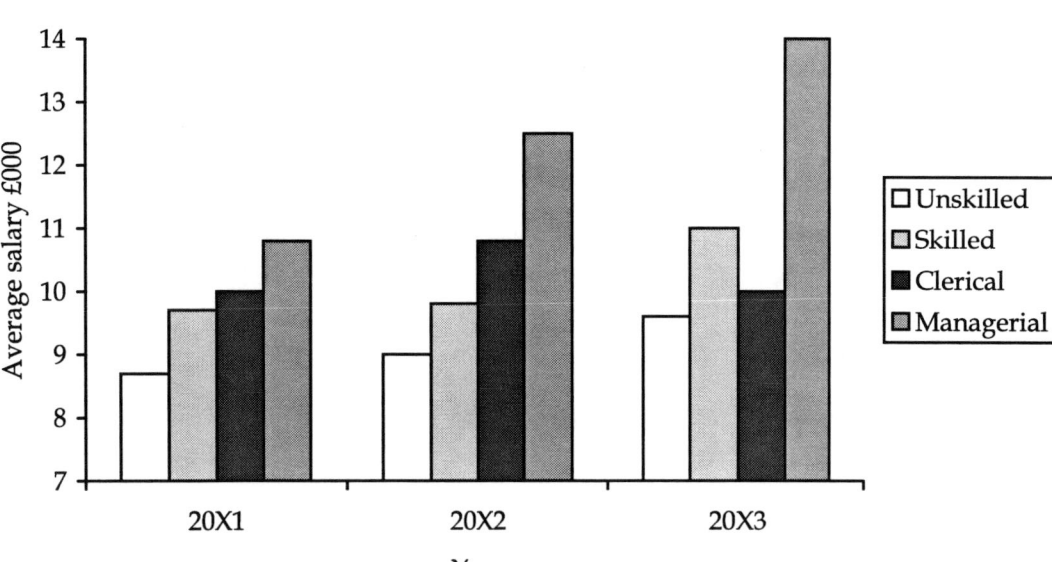

4.8   Solution

♦   The compound bar chart is misleading because the vertical scale does not start from zero (starts presumably from £7,000).

♦   BS Ltd employees are assumed to fall into four categories: unskilled, skilled, clerical and managerial.

♦   All categories of employees had a salary increase each year, except clerical staff in 20X3 when their salaries fell from the previous year. No account was taken of inflation.

♦   The chart is limited in the amount of information it gives since no percentage figures are given. Year to year percentage increases could be calculated for each category by reading figures from the diagram. However, it appears that unskilled and skilled employees have seen about the same percentage increases whilst managerial staff have had much larger percentage increases in salaries.

Activity 5 (The answer is in the final chapter of this book)

BTC (AAT CA J94)

Until three years ago, BTC, an accountancy training organisation, ran its own fleet of vans and delivered manuals to retailers and colleges. The decision was taken to concentrate on core activities and so several organisations were carefully considered before RD plc was selected to take on the responsibility for storing and delivering the manuals. It was agreed that RD would purchase the manuals from BTC at the recommended selling price, less an agreed discount. This ensured that RD would automatically benefit from future increases in the selling price of the manuals. The arrangement has worked well for both organisations and a good relationship has been established.

The managing director of RD has been satisfied with the profits that have been earned, but he is concerned with the efficiency of the transport operation. You, as the assistant accountant, have been asked to provide regular information to the general manager, who is responsible for all aspects of transportation. The general manager has always controlled this area by observing what he calls 'key ratios' which he sees as delivery costs and drivers' wages as a percentage of sales, sales per van and the number of deliveries. He believes that, if these ratios are improving, then the transport operation is working well. He is also a great believer that graphs help to clarify the statistics in any report.

Required

Using the figures from the Appendix below, draw a multiple bar chart (sometimes called a compound bar chart) showing for each year:

(a)   the sales value of the manuals sold

(b)   the van expenses

(c)   the drivers' wages

Appendix

Years	1	2	3
Sales (£)	200,000	222,200	272,630
Van expenses (£)	14,000	15,000	18,000
As percentage of sales	7	6.7	6.6
Drivers' wages (£)	52,000	56,600	68,150
As percentage of sales	26	25.5	25
Number of vans	3	3	4
Sales per van (£)	66,667	74,067	68,158
Number of deliveries	1,000	1,100	1,400

5   Summary

When data is given in narrative form it is often difficult to analyse and understand. However if the narrative data can be shown in tabular form it is often much clearer and easier to understand.

When presenting data in a report it is often appropriate to show the data in the form of a diagram in order that trends or comparisons of component elements can be seen more clearly. Diagrams do not provide precise details of figures but they are useful in providing useful visual information for comparing relative size.

There are a variety of different types of diagram that can be used and the one chosen will depend upon the type of data, the size of the figures and the information that you wish to convey. If the total figures are important a pie chart or percentage component bar chart would not be appropriate but if only the make up of the totals is important then these would be suitable. Therefore care should be taken when choosing which form of diagram to use to illustrate data.

CHAPTER 4

Graphs, time series analysis and index numbers

ASSESSMENT FOCUS

Frequently in assessments you are required to draw a graph to illustrate data. In particular you may be required to graph the results or costs of a business over a number of time periods (a time series) and possibly to find the trend of this series. A further problem that you may need to deal with when comparing results or costs over time is that changing price levels tend to render direct comparison misleading. Therefore you may be required to address this problem by the use of index numbers.

This chapter covers the following Knowledge and Understanding and Performance Criteria of the AAT Syllabus.

> When comparing results over time an appropriate method, which allows for changing price levels, is used (*Performance Criteria element 7.1*)
>
> Time series analysis (*Knowledge and Understanding element 7.1*)
>
> Use of index numbers (*Knowledge and Understanding element 7.1*)

In order to cover these the following topics are included.

> Different types of graphs
>
> How to draw a graph
>
> Time series analysis
>
> Basic trend of a time series
>
> Isolating the trend of a time series using moving averages
>
> Drawing a time series and trend on a graph
>
> Calculating seasonal variations of a time series
>
> Deseasonalisation of time series data
>
> Use of index numbers
>
> Developing an index
>
> Calculating a one item index number
>
> Calculating a weighted index number
>
> Using the retail prices index to deflate a time series

1 Graphs

1.1 Introduction

Graphs are very useful as a means of presenting and interpreting data. Graphs are also very important in **economics** for illustrating, for example, cost and profit functions, and they are often used as a starting point in more **complex statistical analysis**. They are also useful methods of illustrating how costs or revenues have changed over time.

1.2 Straight-line graphs

A straight-line graph is illustrated below.

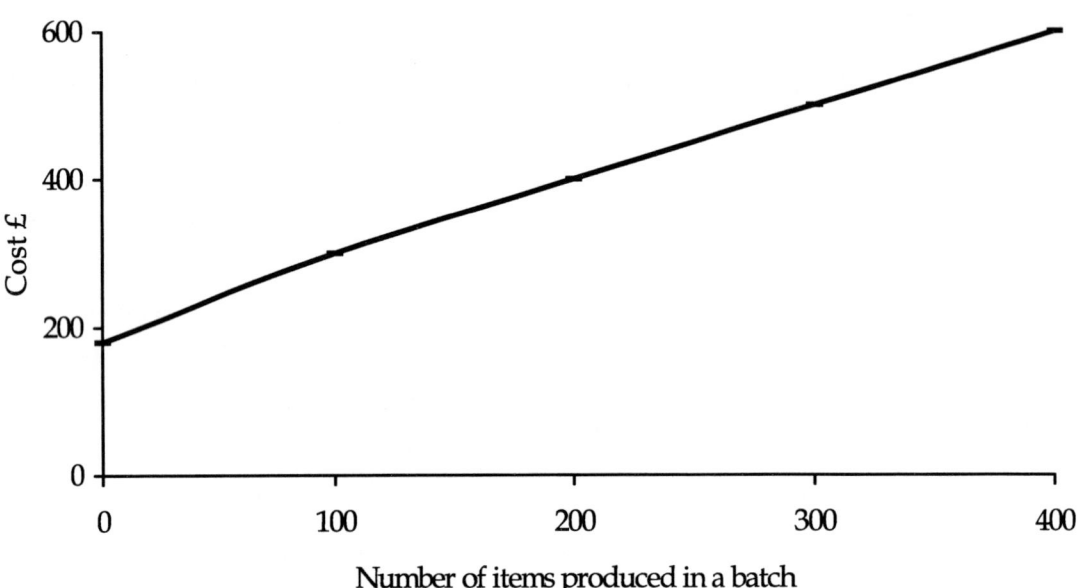

This **straight-line graph** shows the cost of producing a number of items on a production line. It shows that, even if no items are produced, there is a cost of about £190 to 'set up' the production line. After that, costs increase as production increases at a steady rate.

1.3 Time series

Definition A time series is a series of figures given for costs or revenues at regular intervals over time, eg monthly, quarterly, annually. A time series graph is illustrated below.

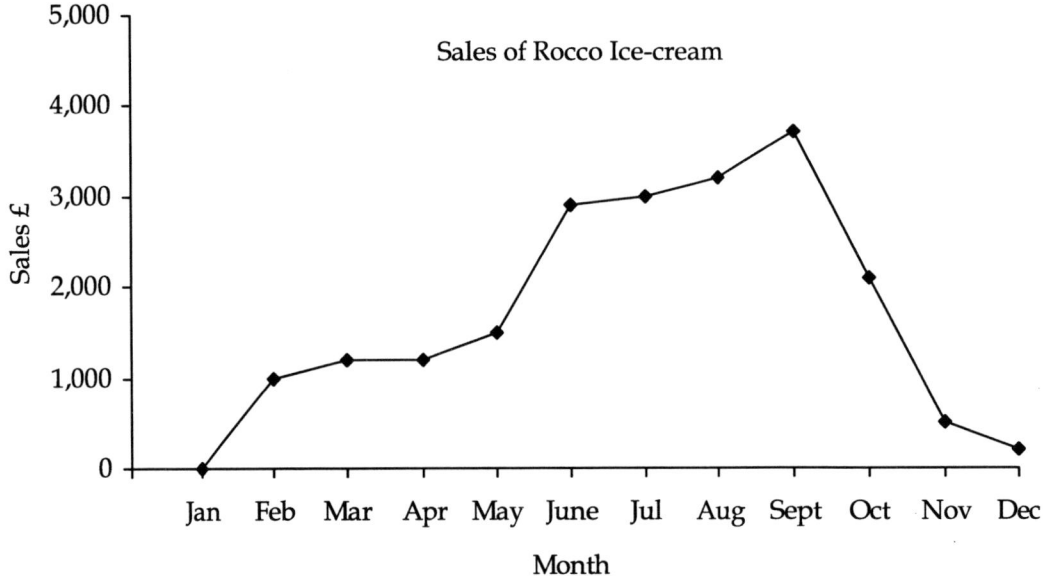

This illustrates the sales of Rocco Ice-cream for the 12 months of a particular year. It shows that, as expected, sales increase over the summer months. The data in such a graph is called a **time series** and is considered in detail later.

 The two graphs shown here are significantly different.

♦ The **straight–line graph** has a clear, direct relationship from which it would be fairly easy to obtain an expression explaining how costs and number of items produced were related.

♦ The pattern shown in the **time series** is more complicated and it would be very difficult to obtain a relationship in this case.

2   How to draw a graph

2.1   Variables

A graph will have just **two variables, x and y,** which are related. The major points to be remembered when drawing such graphs are given below.

 Since there are two variables, two axes are required. The vertical axis is used to represent y, the **dependent variable** in the relationship. The **x variable** is represented on the horizontal axis, this being the **independent variable**. The independent variable is either the time scale with a time series or the factor which causes the change in the dependent variable eg quantity of production.

2.2   Axes

The horizontal and vertical axes are used to represent **both positive and negative values**. This is done by dividing the graph into four quadrants as shown below.

The point where the axes intersect is called the **origin** and is where x = 0 and y = 0. The four quadrants are used for the following values of x and y.

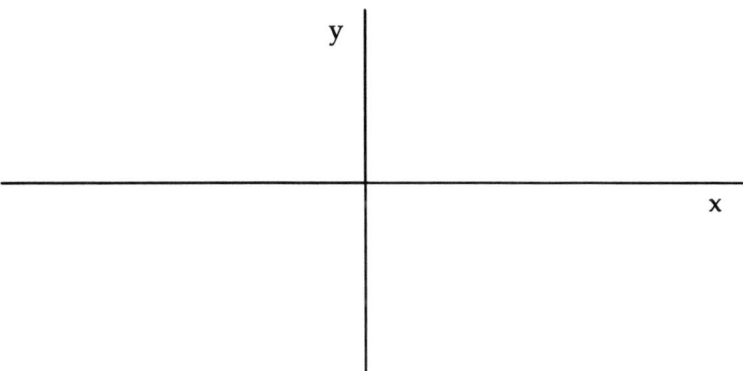

	y	
Second quadrant x negative y positive		First quadrant x positive y positive
Third quadrant x negative y negative		Fourth quadrant x positive y negative

For example, the point   x =   2,   y =   3   falls in the first quadrant

"   x = –2,   y =   3   falls in the second quadrant

"   x = –2,   y = –3   falls in the third quadrant

"   x =   2,   y = –3   falls in the fourth quadrant

 Most graphs that you will be required to draw will be in the first quadrant.

2.3   Scale

Choosing **suitable scales** for the axes is very important. When using graph paper, the squares are divided up in multiples of ten and it is therefore logical to use multiples of ten for the intervals on the scale. It is not practical to use intervals of, say, three or seven on an axis.

 The **intervals for the scales need not be the same** for both the x and y axes. For example, an interval of five units on the x-axis and 100 units on the y-axis is permissible. Care should, however, be taken to examine the scales of the x and y axes when interpreting a graph.

2.4   Labelling the axes

Always remember to **label the axes** on a graph. The minimum requirement is to label them x and y (or some other letters). If the graph has a practical meaning, then label the axes with the actual title of the variable eg production in units on the x axis and total cost on the y axis.

2.5   Example

Draw a graph of the following values:

x	5	–10	–5	–2	10	15
y	50	–100	–50	20	75	25

2.6   Solution

In this data, the x values range from –10 to +15, while the y values range from –100 to +75. Our scales, logically based on intervals of a multiple of 10, must therefore cover these ranges. It would not be sensible in this example to use the same scale for both the x and y axes because of the very different ranges.

A suitable graph is shown below.

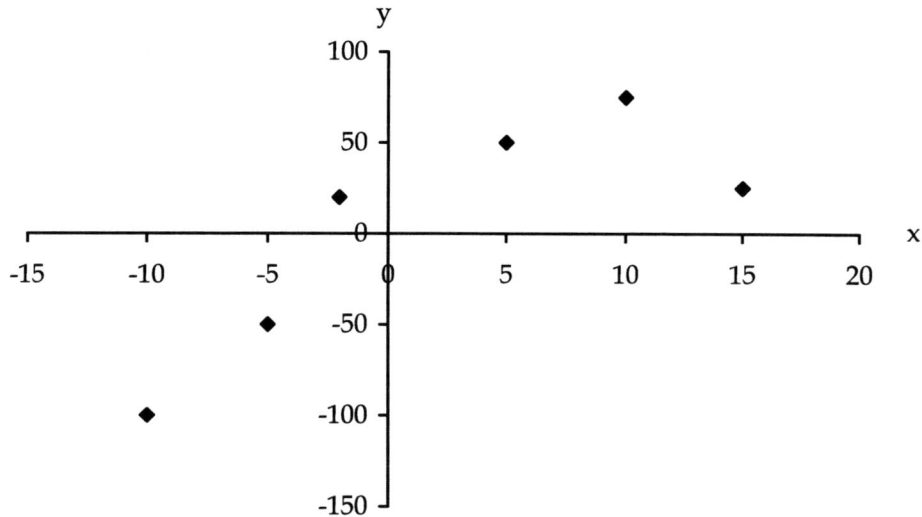

 Take care when planning a graph. Your aim should be to use as much of the page as possible so think carefully about the scale to be used on each axis.

 **Activity 1** *(The answer is in the final chapter of this book)*

Video v DVD

The following data is the number of video recorders/players sold in the United Kingdom from 20X4 to 20X9 inclusive:

Year	20X4	20X5	20X6	20X7	20X8	20X9
Number of video players (millions)	10.61	9.38	8.43	7.37	6.52	5.56

Required

(a)   Plot this data on a graph and comment on the pattern observed.

(b)   The data below gives the number of DVD players sold over the same period:

Year	20X4	20X5	20X6	20X7	20X8	20X9
Number of DVD players (millions)	6.82	8.29	9.57	10.72	11.97	12.71

Is there any evidence to support the statement that the rate of decrease in video players has been compensated for by the increase in DVD players?

3   Time series

3.1   Introduction

Definition   A **time series** is a set of values for some variable (eg monthly production) which varies with time.

The set of observations will be taken at specific times, usually at regular intervals. Examples of figures which can be plotted as a time series are:

(a)   monthly rainfall in London;

(b)   daily closing price of a share on the Stock Exchange;

(c)   weekly sales in a department store.

3.2   Drawing a time series graph

Given below is a typical time series graph representing the quarterly birth rate in the Netherlands over a four year period.

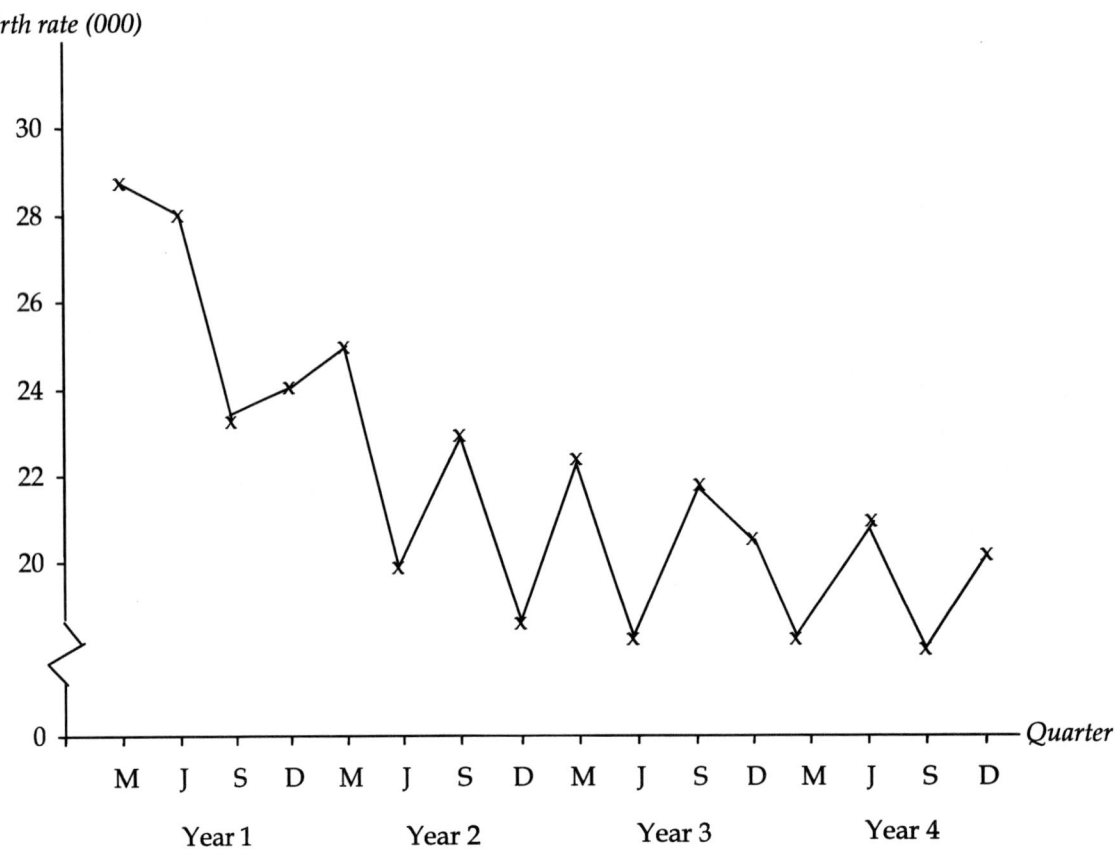

In such a graph, **each point is joined to the next by a straight line,** hence the typically 'jagged' appearance.

Do not make the mistake of trying to construct a smooth curve which will pass through all the points on a time series graph. You will find it practically impossible and, in any case, it is not necessarily correct to do so. In fact, the only reason for joining the points at all is to give a clearer picture of the pattern, which would be more difficult to interpret from a series of dots.

3.3   Use of a time series graph

The **graph of a time series** may be useful for investigating what happened in the past but the real importance of studying a time series is trying to use it to **forecast** what will happen in the future. In other words the past information is recorded, analysed and projected into the future to help with production planning, staff recruitment, etc.

3.4   Characteristic movements of a time series

Analyses of time series have revealed certain characteristic movements or variations, some or all of which are present to varying degrees. These movements are sometimes called the **components** of the time series. Analysis of these components is essential for forecasting purposes. The four main types of components are:

(a)   long-term movements or **basic trend**

(b)   **cyclical** movements;

(c)   **seasonal** movements;

(d)   irregular or **random** movements.

3.5   Basic trend

Definition   The **basic trend** refers to the general direction in which the graph of a time series appears to be going over a long interval of time.

The movement can be represented on the graph by a **trend curve or line**. The trend line is effectively a line of best fit. It is a straight line or curve which best fits the general movement in the time series.

Some common basic trends are illustrated below:

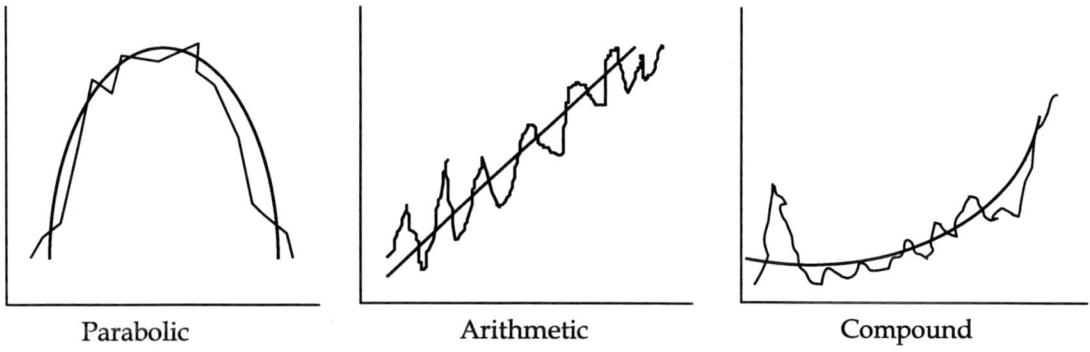

Parabolic   Arithmetic   Compound

3.6   Cyclical variations

Definition   **Cyclical variations** refer to **long-term swings** about the trend line or curve.

These cycles may or may not be periodic, ie they do not necessarily follow exactly similar patterns after equal intervals of time. In business and economic situations movements are said to be cyclical if they recur after time intervals of more than one year. A good example is the trade cycle, representing intervals of prosperity, recession, depression and recovery.

 For cyclical variations to be apparent, data must be available over **very long periods of time** since the periods of oscillation are so long. This is impractical for assessment exercises and for that reason the calculation of cyclical variations is ignored in this chapter although you must, of course, realise that they exist.

3.7   Seasonal variations

Definition   **Seasonal variations** are the identical, or almost identical, patterns which a time series follows during corresponding intervals of successive periods.

Such movements are due to recurring events such as the sudden increase in department store sales before Christmas. Although, in general, seasonal movements refer to a period of one year, this is not always the case and periods of days, hours, weeks, months, etc. may also be considered depending on the type of data available.

3.8   Random variations

Definition   **Random variations** are the sporadic motions of time series due to chance events such as floods, strikes, elections, etc.

Although it is ordinarily assumed that such events produce variations lasting only a short time, it is conceivable that they may be so intense as to result in new cyclical or other movement.

By their very nature they are **unpredictable** and therefore cannot play a large part in any *forecasting* but it is possible to isolate the random variations by calculating all other types of variation and removing them from the time series data. It is important to extract any significant random variations from the data before using them for comparative purposes.

Activity 2 *(The answer is in the final chapter of this book)*

Trends

In what order should the following be placed to show movements that can be described as a trend, seasonal variation, cyclical variation and random variation respectively?

1   The pattern of the number of bed-nights sold by Brighton bed and breakfast establishments.

2   The steady decline in the infant mortality rate due to improvements in intensive care treatment.

3   Changes in house prices in the North relative to the Retail Price Index.

4   The increase in buildings insurance claims due to the worst storms to hit England in history.

A   2, 3, 1, 4

B   2, 1, 3, 4

C   3, 4, 1, 2

D   3, 1, 2, 4

---

4   Time series analysis

4.1   Introduction

The **analysis of a time series** consists of:

(a)   breaking the series down into its **characteristic variations**;

(b)   **projecting** each characteristic into the future;

(c)   adding together all the individual projections to arrive at **one forecast figure** for the complete time series.

The analysis which follows concentrates on isolating only the **basic trend** and **seasonal variations**. As already stated, random movements are not usually included in analysis and, although cyclical movements may be treated in the same way as seasonal variations, they repeat over such long intervals of time that masses of historic data are required before the pattern becomes evident.

4.2   Isolating the trend

One way, admittedly not very scientific, of isolating the trend is **simply to draw it in freehand on the graph** (as with the trend illustration shown earlier in the chapter).

This is not usually good enough for assessment purposes and the two more objective methods are:

(a)   using **moving** averages;

(b)   calculating the least squares line of best fit using **regression analysis**.

However, regression is not covered in this textbook. This section concentrates on the method of **moving averages** which can be used whether the trend is linear or not. This is all that is required for Unit 7.

4.3   Moving averages

Definition   A moving average is an average of each consecutive set of time series figures eg the average of each successive three month period.

By using **moving averages** of **appropriate order**, the variations in a time series can be eliminated leaving a 'smoothed' set of figures which is taken as the trend.

4.4   Example

Given below are the sales figures for a business for the last year.

You are required to calculate a three month moving average for these figures.

Month	Time series sales £000
1	300
2	500
3	500
4	500
5	700
6	900
7	900
8	900
9	1,100
10	1,300
11	1,300
12	1,300

4.5 Solution

Step 1

Calculate the total of the sale for the first three months (month 1 to 3).

$$300 + 500 + 500 = 1{,}300$$

Step 2

Find the average sales for this three month period by dividing by 3.

$$\frac{1{,}300}{3} = 433.33$$

Step 3

Repeat the process for the next three month period (month 2 to 4).

$$\frac{500 + 500 + 500}{3} = 500.00$$

Step 4

Repeat the calculation for each successive three month period.

Month 3 to 5 $\quad \dfrac{500 + 500 + 700}{3} = 566.66$

Month 4 to 6 $\quad \dfrac{500 + 700 + 900}{3} = 700.00$

and so on.

Step 5

List the moving averages on the original time series with each moving average being shown against the middle one of the three months used.

Month	Time series sales £000	3 month moving average £000
1	300	
2	500	433.33
3	500	500.00
4	500	566.66
5	700	700.00
6	900	833.33
7	900	900.00
8	900	966.66
9	1,100	1,100.00
10	1,300	1,233.33
11	1,300	1,300.00
12	1,300	

This three month moving average is the trend of the sales showing a general (and very large) increase over the year.

 A three month moving average would be appropriate where the data appears to have a seasonal pattern (cycle) repeating itself every three months. Each group of three months' data used in the averaging process will contain a representative month from each part of the cycle (e.g. an average month, an above average month and a below average month). Averaging these removes the seasonal effects and shows how the general data movement.

4.6   Centred moving averages

In the previous example the period for the moving average was an odd number ie a three month moving average. This meant that it was possible to place each moving average against the central month for each calculation.

However if the moving average is taken with an even number of periods eg a four year moving average then there is no central period. Instead the moving average total must be shown in the middle of the period which will be between the second and third years of each calculation. This makes it impossible to plot the moving average or trend on a graph.

 Therefore a further average must be taken known as the centred moving average. This is done by taking each successive pairs of moving average figures and finding their own average which is then placed in the middle of their figures. This is the trend figure.

This will all be seen more clearly in the next example.

4.7   Example

Given the following production costs for 20W7–20X7, calculate the four-year moving averages and four-year centred moving averages.

Year	Data £000
20W7	50.0
20W8	36.5
20W9	43.0
20X0	44.5
20X1	38.9
20X2	38.1
20X3	32.6
20X4	38.7
20X5	41.7
20X6	41.1
20X7	38.8

4.8   Solution

Step 1

Calculate the four year moving average for each successive period:

20W7 to 20X0 $\dfrac{50 + 36.5 + 43 + 44.5}{4}$ =   43.5

20W8 to 20X1 $\quad \dfrac{36.5 + 43 + 44.5 + 38.9}{4} \quad = \quad 40.73$

20W9 to 20X2 $\quad \dfrac{43 + 44.5 + 38.9 + 38.1}{4} \quad = \quad 41.13$

and so on.

Step 2

Place each of these figures in the central point of the four year period on the time series ie between the second and third year each time.

Year	Data £000	Four year moving average
20W7	50.0	
20W8	36.5	
		43.50
20W9	43.0	
		40.73
20X0	44.5	
		41.13
20X1	38.9	
		38.53
20X2	38.1	
		37.08
20X3	32.6	
		37.78
20X4	38.7	
		38.53
20X5	41.7	
		40.08
20X6	41.1	
20X7	38.8	

Step 3

Calculate the centred moving average by taking each successive pairs of four year moving averages and finding their average:

$$\dfrac{43.50 + 40.73}{2} = 42.12$$

$$\dfrac{40.73 + 41.13}{2} = 40.93$$

$$\dfrac{41.13 + 38.53}{2} = 39.83$$

and so on.

Step 4

Show each of these centred moving averages in the centre of the two four year figures used – this is effectively against year 3 of each of the original four year's figures used.

Year	Data £000	Four year moving average	Centred moving average Trend
20W7	50.0		
20W8	36.5		
		43.50	
20W9	43.0		42.12
		40.73	
20X0	44.5		40.93
		41.13	
20X1	38.9		39.83
		38.53	
20X2	38.1		37.81
		37.08	
20X3	32.6		37.43
		37.78	
20X4	38.7		38.16
		38.53	
20X5	41.7		39.31
		40.08	
20X6	41.1		
20X7	38.8		

The final column, the centred moving average is the trend of the data. The reason for calculating the centred moving average is so that the trend line can now be plotted on a graph together with the original figures.

Production costs 20W7 to 20X7 and trend

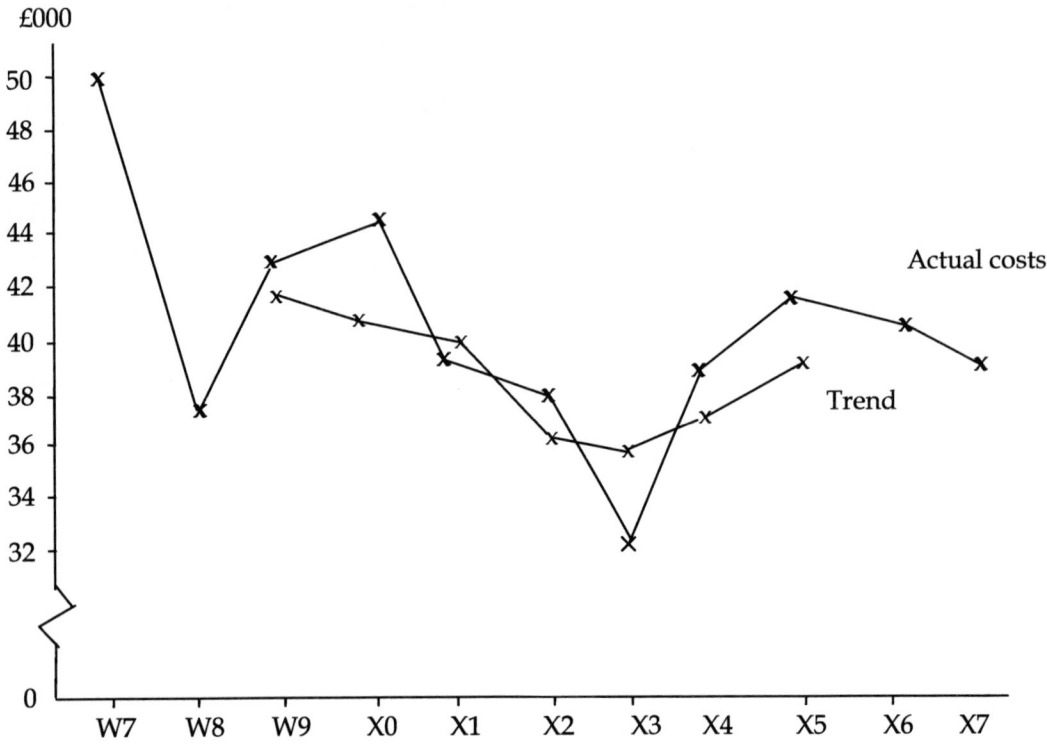

 Note that the vertical axis does not start at zero as the figures are so far above zero. This is perfectly acceptable on a graph provided that the break in the axis shown as above.

 The trend line now clearly depicts what is happening in general with these costs. They fell fairly dramatically and have then started to rise again.

 **Activity 3** *(The answer is in the final chapter of this book)*

Moving average

Sales in £s of a particular product for the last five years have been:

100, 110, 108, 112, 107

Calculate a three-year moving average to the nearest £.

4.9   *Disadvantages of moving averages*

Although an extremely simple method of finding the trend, moving averages have certain **disadvantages**.

(a)   **Data at the beginning and end of the series is lost** – therefore the moving averages do not cover the complete period.

(b)   The moving averages may generate **cycles or other movements** that were not present in the original data.

(c)   The averages are **strongly affected by extreme values**. To overcome this a 'weighted' moving average is sometimes used giving the largest weights to central items and small weights to extreme values.

4.10   Seasonal variations

Having isolated the trend, a method is needed to deal with the seasonal variations.

The workings which follow are based on an **additive time series model**. This states that the four components of a time series (T = trend; S = seasonal variation; C = cyclical variation; R = random variation) are expressed as **absolute values which are simply added together to produce the actual figures.**

ie Actual data = T + S + C + R

For unsophisticated analysis over a relatively short period of time C and R are ignored.

♦   **Random variations are ignored** because they are unpredictable and would not normally exhibit any repetitive pattern

♦   **Cyclical variations** (long term oscillations) are ignored because their effect is negligible over short periods of time.

The model therefore simplifies to:

A (actual data) = T + S (trend + seasonal variations)

Thus, in the **additive model** seasonal variations are expressed in absolute terms with above and below average figures designated by plus and minus signs respectively. The method can be based on a trend produced by any method.

4.11   Calculating the seasonal variation

The **seasonal variation,** if we are ignoring cyclical and random variations, is simply the **difference between the actual data and the trend.** Rearranging the above equation gives:

Seasonal variations, S = Actual data – Trend

or,   S = A – T

4.12   Example

Consider the following sales figures.

Year/Quarter	1	2	3	4
1	74	100	94	127
2	84	106	120	141
3	94	112	130	147
4	112	118	148	169
5	138	140		

Calculate the trend and seasonal variation and then deseasonalise the data.

4.13 *Solution*

Step 1: Calculate the trend and then the seasonal variation

		(a) Data	(b) 4–quarter moving average	(c) Centred moving average Trend (T)	(d) Seasonal variation (S) (a) –(c)
1	1	74			
	2	100			
			98.75		
	3	94		100	(6)
			101.25		
	4	127		102	25
			102.75		
2	1	84		106	(22)
			109.25		
	2	106		111	5
			112.75		
	3	120		114	6
			115.25		
	4	141		116	25
			116.75		
3	1	94		118	(24)
			119.25		
	2	112		120	(8)
			120.75		
	3	130		123	7
			125.25		
	4	147		126	21
			126.75		
4	1	112		129	(17)
			131.25		
	2	118		134	(16)
			136.75		
	3	148		140	8
			143.25		
	4	169		146	23
			148.75		
5	1	138			
	2	140			

Step 2: Calculate the average seasonal variations

Tabulating the variations for each quarter and finding their averages, quarter by quarter, should eliminate some of the effects of random variations.

Year/Quarter	1	2	3	4
1	–	–	(6)	25
2	(22)	5	6	25
3	(24)	(8)	7	21
4	(17)	(16)	8	23
5	–	–	–	–
Sum	(63)	(19)	15	94
Average	(21)	(6)	3.75	23.5

The purpose of the averaging shown above is to find one representative seasonal variation for each quarter. This will then enable both **forecasting** and **deseasonalisation of the original data** to be carried out. Strictly speaking the sum of these four average variations should be zero (it is actually 0.25). It is customary to add (0.25 ÷ 4 = 0.0625) to each average figure to adjust for this (but as the figures are so small in this case we will ignore this).

Step 3: Deseasonalisation of data

Having isolated the seasonal variations, the original data can be deseasonalised by removing these variations. It is customary, when quoting **government statistics**, to quote deseasonalised ('seasonally adjusted') figures . . . when it is deemed convenient! After data have been deseasonalised they still include trend, cyclical and random movements. The trend has already been found and can now be removed from the deseasonalised data to leave only cyclical and random movements (residual variations).

Year & quarter		*(a)* Data	*(e)* Average seasonal variations	*(f)* Deseasonalised data *(a) – (e)*	*(c)* Trend *(as before)*	*(g)* Residual variations (cyclical & random) *(f) – (c)*
1	3	94	3.75	90.25	100	(9.75)
	4	127	23.50	103.50	102	1.50
2	1	84	(21.00)	105.00	106	(1.00)
	2	106	(6.00)	112.00	111	1.00
	3	120	3.75	116.25	114	2.25
	4	141	23.50	117.50	116	1.50
3	1	94	(21.00)	115.00	118	(3.00)
	2	112	(6.00)	118.00	120	(2.00)
	3	130	3.75	126.25	123	3.25
	4	147	23.50	123.50	126	(2.50)
4	1	112	(21.00)	133.00	129	4.00
	2	118	(6.00)	124.00	134	(10.00)
	3	148	3.75	144.25	140	4.25
	4	169	23.50	145.50	146	(0.50)

4.14 Example

The following data shows the number of cash receipts per day for a company over four working weeks:

Week/day	1	2	3	4	5
1	8	12	15	10	9
2	10	13	17	15	16
3	17	23	25	21	21
4	26	30	32	34	35

Plot the data on a graph. Calculate the trend using five-day moving averages and superimpose this trend on your graph. What are the seasonal variations and the residual variations?

4.15 Solution

The five-day moving average trend is simply found by adding up the figures in fives and dividing by five. No centring is required as the moving average is based on an odd number.

Week/day		(a) Data	(b) 5 day moving average Trend	(c) Seasonal variation (a) – (b)	(d) Average seasonal variations (working)	(e) Deseasonalised data (a) – (d)	(f) Residual variations (e) – (b)
1	1	8					
	2	12					
	3	15	10.8	4.2	2.8	12.2	1.4
	4	10	11.2	(1.2)	(1.3)	11.3	0.1
	5	9	11.4	(2.4)	(2.5)	11.5	0.1
2	1	10	11.8	(1.8)	(1.3)	11.3	(0.5)
	2	13	12.8	0.2	1.4	11.6	(1.2)
	3	17	14.2	2.8	2.8	14.2	0
	4	15	15.6	(0.6)	(1.3)	16.3	0.7
	5	16	17.6	(1.6)	(2.5)	18.5	0.9
3	1	17	19.2	(2.2)	(1.3)	18.3	(0.9)
	2	23	20.4	2.6	1.4	21.6	1.2
	3	25	21.4	3.6	2.8	22.2	0.8
	4	21	23.2	(2.2)	(1.3)	22.3	(0.9)
	5	21	24.6	(3.6)	(2.5)	23.5	(1.1)
4	1	26	26.0	0	(1.3)	27.3	1.3
	2	30	28.6	1.4	1.4	28.6	0
	3	32	31.4	0.6	2.8	29.2	(2.2)
	4	34					
	5	35					

Seasonal variations

Week/day	1	2	3	4	5
1	–	–	4.2	(1.2)	(2.4)
2	(1.8)	0.2	2.8	(0.6)	(1.6)
3	(2.2)	2.6	3.6	(2.2)	(3.6)
4	0	1.4	0.6	–	–
Sum	(4.0)	4.2	11.2	(4.0)	(7.6)
Average	(1.3)	1.4	2.8	(1.3)	(2.5)

The trend values and the actual receipts are then plotted on a graph.

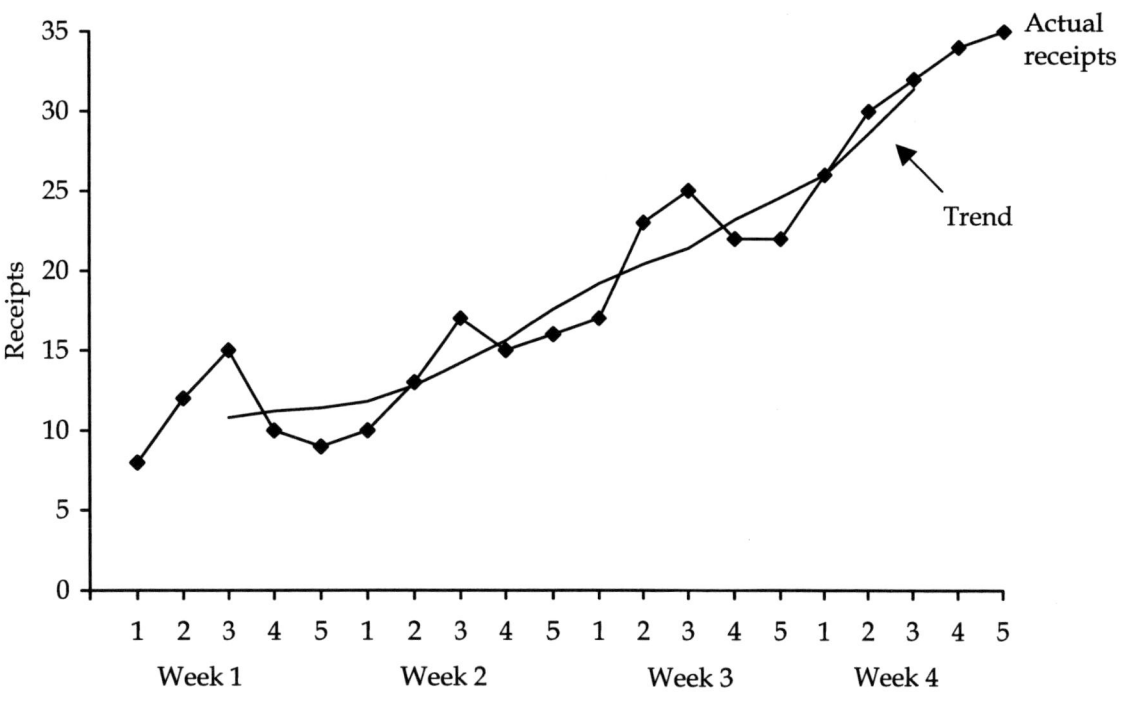

Activity 4 *(The answer is in the final chapter of this book)*

Movements

Explain the four characteristic movements of a time series. With which characteristic movement would you mainly associate each of the following?

(i)   A fire in a factory delaying production for three weeks?

(ii)   An era of prosperity?

(iii) An after Easter sale in a department store?

(iv)   A need for increased wheat production due to a constant increase in population?

(v)   The monthly number of inches of rainfall in a city over a five-year period?

(vi)   A recession?

(vii) An increase in employment during summer months?

(viii) The decline in the death rate due to advances in science?

(ix)   A steel strike?

(x)   A continually increasing demand for smaller cars?

4.16   *Making a forecast using a time series*

If you are required to forecast a figure for the future given a time series, there are three main ways of doing it:

♦ drawing the time series, drawing in a trend line and extending it in the direction it appears to be going

♦ looking at the increment between trend values and seeing if there is a pattern; if there is, add on values for this pattern until your required date in the future is reached.

♦ if there is no patterns in the increment, calculate an average increment and add these on until you reach the date.

Note that however you use a time series to predict a value in the future, you cannot predict very far ahead.

5 Index numbers

5.1 Introduction

 **Definition**   An **index number** is a means of explaining changes over time in economic variables such as prices, wages, output, etc.

It shows how these items **change with time** and can be divided into three types:

(a)   **price index numbers**, which measure changes in prices;

(b)   **quantity index numbers**, which measure changes in quantity;

(c)   **value index numbers**, which measure changes in the value of services or activities of goods.

5.2 Using an index

 An index is a useful method of comparing figures over time by simplifying them to a single index figure that can be compared to a base year which is given an index of 100. The index then shows the change in the figures each year comparison to that base year.

5.3 Example

Given below are the production cost figures for a business for the last eight years:

Year	Cost £000
20X0	138
20X1	149
20X2	158
20X3	130
20X4	136
20X5	150
20X6	154
20X7	162

You are to calculate an index for these costs using 20X0 as the base year.

5.4 Solution

The formula for calculation of each year's index is $\dfrac{\text{Current year costs}}{\text{Base year costs}} \times 100$.

We can now calculate the index for each year:

Year	Cost £000	Calculation	Index
20X0	138	$138/138 \times 100$	100.0
20X1	149	$149/138 \times 100$	108.0
20X2	158	$158/138 \times 100$	114.5
20X3	130	$130/138 \times 100$	94.2
20X4	136	$136/138 \times 100$	98.6
20X5	150	$150/138 \times 100$	108.7
20X6	154	$154/138 \times 100$	111.6
20X7	162	$162/138 \times 100$	117.4

 The indices that are above 100 show that the costs have increased over the 20X0 costs in that year. The indices that are below 100 show that the costs are lower in that year than in 20X0.

We can now see clearly from the index figures that costs rose for two years then fell below 20X0 levels for two years before continuing to rise substantially.

6 Developing an index

6.1 Introduction

The general problems found in developing an index are as follows.

♦   Selection of items to be included.

♦   Choice of base year.

♦   Choice of weights if the index is an aggregate.

6.2 Items to be included

The items to be included in the index should be: (1) **relevant**, (2) **representative**, (3) **reliable** and (4) **comparable over time**.

(1)   Items must be **relevant**, eg a producers' price index should be composed of wholesale prices, whereas a cost of living index should comprise retail prices.

(2)   An index number is generally based on a sample. For example, it would be impossible to include prices for every type of food in an index of food prices. The items chosen should be adequate in number and importance and **representative of the whole**. Generally the index will be more reliable the more items there are, as abnormal movements in one or two commodities will not unduly affect it.

(3)   It is essential for the data to **be accurate**. Preference should be given to items for which reliable quotations can be obtained with confidence.

(4)   One of the greatest difficulties is **variation in quality or situations** where the classification of the item has changed.

6.3 Base period

Because the trend represents a movement in prices there has to be a **base period** to compare with. The year or period chosen for a base must be 'normal', eg. if constructing an index to measure the volume of motor car production, the base month should not be one in which there was a major strike. This would give a misleading impression of the prosperity of the motor industry if the months following the strike showed a substantial increase.

The base period may be a single date, a month or a year. The **length of the base period** usually depends on the interval at which the index number is to be calculated. The index number for the base period is given the value 100 and this might be allocated to :

♦ a year – 20X5 = 100;

♦ a month – August 20X5 = 100;

♦ a single date – 16 August 20X5 = 100.

6.4   *Relatives, or one item index numbers*

If the price of one item is recorded at different times, then an index number can be constructed to show **changes in price**.

The index number, or price relative is $\dfrac{\text{Current price of item}}{\text{Base price of item}} \times 100.$

6.5   *Example*

Year	Price of car service
20X0	£36.50
20X1	£39.20
20X2	£44.70
20X3	£51.40
20X4	£52.50

Taking 20X1 as the base year calculate an index for these prices.

6.6   *Solution*

The index for 20X0 is:

$$\frac{36.50}{39.20} \times 100 = 93.1$$

Similarly, for 20X2:

$$\frac{44.70}{39.20} \times 100 = 114.0$$

and if the other years' index numbers are calculated:

20X3 $\dfrac{51.40}{39.20} \times 100 = 131.1$

20X4 $\dfrac{52.50}{39.20} \times 100 = 133.9$

6.7   Using the index

 The figures obtained are index numbers and often called **price relatives**. All the figures are calculated as percentages of the figure for 20X1 and so they show percentage changes from 20X1 (eg the price for 20X3 is 31.1% higher than that in 20X1).

However, you cannot say the percentage rise from 20X3 to 20X4 is:

133.9 – 131.1 = 2.8%

It is in fact:

$$\frac{52.50}{51.40} \times 100 \ = \ 102.1$$

so a 2.1% increase has occurred. We could use the appropriate index numbers to find this increase from 20X3 to 20X4:

$$\frac{133.9}{131.1} \times 100 \ = \ 102.1 \ \ (\text{as before})$$

6.8   Quantity index

The idea of a relative or single item index is not limited to prices. Suppose the number of cars serviced at a garage is known. Then, an index with base year 20X1 is calculated as:

Year	Number of cars	Index number	
20X0	2,138	$\frac{2{,}138}{2{,}210} \times 100 =$	96.7
20X1	2,210		100.0
20X2	2,356	$\frac{2{,}356}{2{,}210} \times 100 =$	106.6
20X3	2,199	$\frac{2{,}199}{2{,}210} \times 100 =$	99.5
20X4	2,056	$\frac{2{,}056}{2{,}210} \times 100 =$	93.0

This is called a **quantity index**.

6.9   Aggregates, or weighted index numbers

The more complex situation is where **several items need to be combined into a single index number**.

6.10   Example

A firm's production involves three raw materials, the unit costs of which are:

	Costs (per kg) 20X3	*Costs (per kg) 20X4*
Steel	£2.00	£2.50
Plastics	£1.50	£1.50
Wood	£0.50	£0.60

To compare costs we would average these costs and then work out an index number comparing those average costs. This, however, does not take account of the fact that different quantities of each raw material may be required. If 3 kg of steel, 2 kg of plastic and 1 kg of wood are used, then a weighted index is found using the quantities as weightings.

The formula for a weighted index is:

Combined index number $= \dfrac{\text{Weighted average for given period}}{\text{Weighted average for base period}} \times 100$

and the weighted average is calculated in the usual way as:

Weighted average $= \dfrac{\Sigma wx}{\Sigma w}$

where x denotes costs and w denotes weights.

Calculate an index for 20X4 with 20X3 as the base year (20X3 index = 100).

6.11 Solution

Raw material		w	20X3 costs	wx_3	20X4	wx_4
			£	£	£	£
Steel		3	2.00	6.00	2.50	7.50
Plastics		2	1.50	3.00	1.50	3.00
Wood		1	0.50	0.50	0.60	0.60
	Σw	6		Σwx_3 9.50		Σwx_4 11.10

Weighted average (20X3) $= \dfrac{£9.50}{6} = £1.5833$

Weighted average (20X4) $= \dfrac{£11.10}{6} = £1.8500$

The index is then:

20X3 $= 100.0$

20X4 $\dfrac{1.8500}{1.5833} \times 100 = 116.8$

This could also be computed as:

$= \dfrac{\Sigma wx_4}{\Sigma w_3} \times 100 = \dfrac{11.10}{9.50} \times 100 = 116.8$

This is known as an aggregative approach to calculating a weighted index.

6.12   Example

(a)   Find an index number for 20X3 and 20X4 with 20X2 as base period for average pay using the figures in the table and an aggregative approach.

Average pay (£)

	20X2 £	20X3 £	20X4 £
Non-skilled	110	115	123
Semi-skilled	128	145	162
Skilled	150	162	180

There are 25 non-skilled, 15 semi-skilled and 10 skilled employees.

(b)   What is the percentage rise in average pay from 20X2 to 20X3 and from 20X3 to 20X4?

6.13   Solution

(a)   Using the numbers of employees as weights the calculations are:

	w	Pay (20X2) £	$w \times pay$ £
Non-skilled	25	110	2,750
Semi-skilled	15	128	1,920
Skilled	10	150	1,500
	50		6,170

20X2 weighted average = $\dfrac{£6,170}{50}$ = £123.4

	w	Pay (20X3) £	$w \times pay$ £
Non-skilled	25	115	2,875
Semi-skilled	15	145	2,175
Skilled	10	162	1,620
	50		6,670

20X3 weighted average = $\dfrac{£6,670}{50}$ = £133.4

	w	Pay (20X4) £	$w \times pay$ £
Non-skilled	25	123	3,075
Semi-skilled	15	162	2,430
Skilled	10	180	1,800
	50		7,305

20X4 weighted average = $\dfrac{£7,305}{50}$ = £146.1

The index number is then (using 20X2 as base year = 100):

Year	Index
20X2	100.0
20X3	$\dfrac{133.4}{123.4} \times 100 = 108.1$
20X4	$\dfrac{146.1}{123.4} \times 100 = 118.4$

(b)   To find the percentage increase from 20X2, the base year, simply take the difference in the index number value. For 20X3 it is:

% Rise from 20X2 to 20X3 =   108.1 – 100   =   8.1%

However, to find the change from 20X3 to 20X4, as 20X3 is not the base year, work out the index number ratio and subtract 100, ie:

% Rise from 20X3 to 20X4 $= \left(\dfrac{118.4}{108.1} \times 100\right) - 100 = 109.5 - 100 = 9.5\%$

Activity 5 *(The answer is in the final chapter of this book)*

WBA

The cost of the materials used in the manufacturing of a technical manual, WBA, is:

	20X3			20X4		
	Quantity	*Price*	*Pence*	*Quantity*	*Price*	*Pence*
Cover	1	10.8p	10.8	1	10.6	10.6
Paper	230	30p/100	69	250	31p/100	77.5
Ink	5	1p	5	6	1p	6
Bindings	1	2p	2	1	3p	3
			86.8			97.1

Calculate an index number which indicates the overall change in prices in 20X4 (20X3 = 100). Use 20X3 quantities as the basis for the calculation.

6.14   Retail Prices Index (RPI)

One of the most commonly used indices is the Retail Prices Index. This is an index compiled by the Department of Employment and published monthly in the Department of Employment Gazette and Monthly Digest of Statistics.

Definition   The **general index of retail prices** measures the percentage changes month by month in the average level of prices of commodities and services purchased by the great majority of households in the UK, including practically all wage earners and most small and medium salary earners.

The RPI is often used as a measure of general inflation in the country.

6.15   Deflating a series using the Retail Prices Index (RPI)

If a series of figures is concerned with **sums of money** and **recorded through time** then it will be affected by **inflation** and so changes can be misleading. One often hears comments such as '£1.50 for a pint of beer! It was only 2s 4d when I was a boy'. The important factor is, how long did someone have to work to earn the 2s 4d to buy the original pint and how long does he now have to work to buy the current pint?

To overcome this, **'real prices' are found by deflating the original series**. This is effectively changing the money values to values at one point in time, the base time, and so making the figures directly comparable.

6.16   Example

Consider the following table of average weekly pay and the RPI, by year:

Year	Average weekly wage £	RPI
20X5	69.50	91.0
20X6	78.40	98.6
20X7	90.10	111.8
20X8	108.60	131.9
20X9	120.30	145.9

6.17   Solution

The 'real' value of earnings in relation to 20X5 would be calculated as:

$$\text{Average wage for year} \times \frac{\text{RPI for 20X5}}{\text{RPI for year}}$$

This gives for 20X6, a deflated figure of:

$$£78.40 \times \frac{91.0}{98.6} = £72.36$$

Similarly, for 20X7 the deflated figure is:

$$£90.10 \times \frac{91.0}{111.8} = £73.34$$

For 20X8 the deflated figure is:

$$£108.60 \times \frac{91.0}{131.9} = £74.92$$

and for 20X9 the deflated figure is:

$$£120.30 \times \frac{91.0}{145.9} = £75.03$$

Bringing this information together in one table, gives:

Year	Average weekly wage £	RPI	'Real' weekly wage (20X5) £
20X5	69.50	91.0	69.50
20X6	78.40	98.6	72.36
20X7	90.10	111.8	73.34
20X8	108.60	131.9	74.92
20X9	120.30	145.9	75.03

Looking at the change from 20X5 to 20X9 shows that the purchasing power of average wages has risen by:

$$\frac{75.03 - 69.50}{69.50} \times 100$$

$$= \frac{5.53}{69.50} \times 100 = 7.96\%$$

Use of the RPI to deflate figures for costs or revenues is often used in assessments in order to give a more realistic picture of any changes in costs and revenues.

Activity 6 *(The answer is in the final chapter of this book)*

Energy supplies

Given below is the sales revenue of a business from 20X1 to 20X5 and the average RPI for each year.

Year	Sales £	RPI
20X1	486,000	111.8
20X2	521,000	131.9
20X3	562,000	145.9
20X4	604,000	150.3
20X5	683,000	156.3

Required

(a)   Deflate the sales revenue using the RPI to show all revenue in terms of 20X1 prices.

(b)   Comment on your results.

7   Summary

In this chapter we have been considering cost and revenue information over a period of time. This is known as a time series and the costs or revenues can be illustrated on a graph.

Further analysis can then be made of this time series by firstly isolating the basic trend by calculating moving averages. The basic trend line can then be drawn onto the time series graph to indicate how the figures are generally moving over time. A further element of time series analysis is to find the seasonal variations by comparing the actual figures to the trend figure. Once the average seasonal variation is taken out of the actual figures they are known as deseasonalised or seasonally adjusted figures.

When comparing a list of figures for costs, revenues or quantities over time it is not always easy to determine how these figures are moving. Use of an index for each period's figures compared to a base period index of 100 shows quite clearly whether each period's figures are increasing or decreasing compared to the base period.

One further specific use of an index is to use the Retail Prices Index, the general measure of price inflation, to deflate a time series in order that any real increase or decrease in costs or revenues can be clearly seen.

CHAPTER 5

Performance assessment

ASSESSMENT FOCUS

In assessments you are likely to have to produce a number of performance indicators for organisational units (eg divisions) indicating levels of profitability, measures of cost per unit, productivity and resource utilisation. You may also have to deal with the simple consolidation of figures for different divisions or companies within the organisation and any trading that has taken place between them.

This chapter covers the following Knowledge and Understanding and Performance Criteria of the AAT Syllabus.

Information derived from different units of the organisation is consolidated into the appropriate form (*Performance Criteria element 7.1*)

Information derived from different information systems within the organisation is correctly reconciled (*Performance Criteria element 7.1*)

Transactions between separate units of the organisation are accounted for in accordance with the organisation's procedures (*Performance Criteria element 7.1*)

Ratios and performance indicators are accurately calculated in accordance with the organisation's procedures (*Performance Criteria element 7.1*)

Ratios and performance indicators are accurately calculated in accordance with the organisation's procedures (*Performance Criteria element 7.1*)

Use of standard units of inputs and outputs (*Knowledge and Understanding elements 7.1, 7.3*)

Calculations of ratios and performance indicators are accurate (*Knowledge and Understanding element 7.2*)

Awareness of relevant performance and quality measures (*Knowledge and Understanding element 7.1*)

Main types of performance indicators: productivity; cost per unit; resource utilisation; profitability (*Knowledge and Understanding element 7.2*)

Ratios: gross profit margin; net profit margin; return on capital employed (*Knowledge and Understanding elements 7.1, 7.2*)

In order to cover these the following topics are included.

Cost per unit

Productivity measures

Resource utilisation

Profitability ratios

Interpretation of ratios

Dealing with divisions and divisional reporting

Transactions between divisions

Consolidation of divisional results

1 Analysing performance

1.1 Types of analysis

A common type of internal management report will be an **analysis of performance** in some respect. Examples might include the following:

♦ **Performance of individual units within the business** – divisions, departments, services, products, processes or sales areas.

   Performance indicators will depend upon the nature of the unit. For example, divisions and products may be measured in terms of profitability, services and processes in terms of costs per unit, productivity and/or resource utilisation measures.

♦ **Overall performance of the organisation as a whole,** in comparison with budgeted targets, previous years and/or other organisations in the same business sector.

   Performance indicators in this instance will commonly be in terms of profitability and resource utilisation. Measures will often be in the form of **ratios**.

In addition, **returns to outside agencies**, such as trade associations, will often require various ratios, percentages and other performance indicators for the returning organisation (see next chapter).

1.2 Performance indicators

This chapter looks at the most **common performance indicators** and how they might be applied to various types of business. The performance indicators to be covered are:

♦ Cost per unit

♦ Productivity

♦ Resource utilisation

♦ Profitability

1.3 Organisational units

The syllabus for Unit 7 also requires you to be able to deal with different units within an organisation eg divisions, subsidiary companies. Therefore we will consider how to consolidate the figures for different organisational units.

2 Costs per unit

2.1 Introduction

A common method of assessing the performance of a part of the organisation for which costs can be separately ascertained is to measure the **cost per unit**.

2.2 Cost units

The determination of an **appropriate cost unit** for the particular activity or part of the business being assessed can be difficult, but is key to giving a meaningful measure. The cost unit chosen should relate to the relevant output or activity in such a way that it is clear that levels of costs will in some way be dependent upon the level of cost unit.

We will now think about examples for different types of business and activity.

2.3 Manufacturing businesses or processes

Production and related costs will invariably be related to the **products being produced/sold.** Thus the cost unit will also be directly derived from the product units themselves.

Business/process	*Cost unit*
Book publisher	Book
Printing process	1,000 pages printed
Brewing	Barrel
Electricity	kWh (ie kilowatt hour)
Timber mill	100 ft of wood

2.4 Non-manufacturing businesses/activities

These present greater problems in determining a suitable standard measure of output or activity. Some examples of commonly used cost units for **service industries, or service departments** within a business, are given below; however, there will often be equally useful alternatives.

Business/activity	*Cost unit*
Accountants	Chargeable hour
College	Enrolled student
Hotel	Bed-night
Hospital	Patient-day
Credit control	Customer account
Selling	Orders taken/£ sales made
Maintenance	Man-hours

2.5 Allocation of costs to cost units

To determine the cost per unit, the particular product, area of business or activity will need to have **costs attributed to it,** both direct costs and overheads. The process of tracing costs to cost units via these 'cost centres' will include **overhead allocation, apportionment and absorption,** as assessed in Unit 6.

 You are unlikely to be asked to get involved in complex cost-tracing exercises for this unit; you may, however, have to decide upon an appropriate cost unit over which to spread given costs.

2.6 Example

A production process has incurred costs of £124,000 for the week ending 30 September 20X0. During that week it produced 200,000 of its single product.

What is the cost per unit produced?

2.7 Solution

$$\text{Cost per unit} = \frac{£124,000}{200,000} = 62 \text{ pence per unit}$$

Activity 1 *(The answer is in the final chapter of this book)*

Haulage accounting unit

Suggest suitable cost units appropriate to the following:

(a)   a road haulage business

(b)   a firm of solicitors

(c)   a hospital

3   Productivity

3.1   Introduction

Productivity is a measure of the efficiency of the production process or service provision within an organisation. It can be measured in a variety of ways but is normally measured as a ratio.

3.2   Labour productivity

One common method of measuring the productivity of the labour force is to calculate the number of units produced for each direct labour hour and then to compare this to the budgeted production per labour hour. The units per direct labour hour can also be compared over time by looking at the productivity in each period.

3.3   Example

The budget for a factory is to produce 120,000 units of its single product in a week using 24,000 direct labour hours The actual production in the week was 116,000 units and this took 24,500 hours.

What is the actual level of output per direct labour hour for the week and how does this compare to the budgeted level of output?

3.4   Solution

$$\text{Actual output per direct labour hour} = \frac{116,000 \text{ units}}{24,500} = 4.73 \text{ units per hour}$$

$$\text{Budgeted output per direct labour hour} = \frac{120,000 \text{ units}}{24,000} = 5 \text{ units per hour}$$

Therefore the productivity of the factory for the week is lower than the budgeted productivity.

3.5   Labour efficiency

The efficiency of the labour force can be measured by comparing the expected hours for the actual production to the actual hours worked. This is normally expressed as a percentage.

$$\text{Efficiency} = \frac{\text{Budgeted hours for actual production}}{\text{Actual hours for actual production}} \times 100$$

3.6   Example

The budget for a factory is to produce 120,000 units of its single product in a week using 24,000 direct labour hours. The actual production in the week was 116,000 units and this took 24,500 hours.

What is the labour efficiency measure for the week?

3.7   Solution

$$\text{Efficiency} = \frac{\text{Budgeted hours for actual production}}{\text{Actual hours for actual production}} \times 100$$

As it was budgeted that 5 units should be produced each hour then the budgeted hours for the actual production of 116,000 units should be:

$$\frac{116,000}{5} = 23,200 \text{ hours}$$

$$\text{Efficiency} = \frac{23,200}{24,500} \times 100$$

$$= 94.7\%$$

As this figure is less than 100% it shows a lack of efficiency from the workforce compared to the budgeted figures.

3.8   Machine productivity

In a machine intensive production environment it may also be useful to calculate the number of units produced per machine hour. This can then be compared to the budgeted production per machine hour or to the production levels of earlier periods.

3.9   Example

A machine production line was in operation for 48 hours in the week ending 24 July 20X0 and 1,200 units were produced. In the previous week the production line was in operation for 45 hours and 1,150 units were produced.

Compare the machine productivity for the two weeks.

3.10   Solution

Week ending 24 July $\quad \dfrac{1,200}{48} \quad = \quad$ 25 units per machine hour

Previous week $\quad \dfrac{1,150}{45} \quad = \quad$ 25.5 units per machine hour

The current week's production is less efficient than the previous week.

3.11   Non-manufacturing organisations

Productivity measures can also be used in non-manufacturing organisations or business units. For example in a firm of accountants the number of chargeable hours per professional staff member may be calculated and monitored. In a sales department the number of sales orders taken per sales staff each week may be calculated.

It is important to realise that the calculation of any of these performance indicators on their own is not enough. The performance indicators are only of use if they are compared either over time or between divisions or to budgeted figures.

Activity 2 *(The answer is in the final chapter of this book)*

The Snowy Ski Company

Data

The Snowy Ski Company manufacture skis and related equipment. Charles O'Hagan is manager of the main factory based in South Wales. There is a second factory in Yorkshire, England. The production department is made up of the following sections.

◆ Moulding

◆ Assembly

◆ Finishing

Mr O'Hagan has become concerned about the performance of his workforce compared with the factory in Yorkshire. He has collected performance data from the two factories and produced a spreadsheet model to analyse the data. The results of this data are given below.

You are an accounting technician, assisting Mr O'Hagan in the South Wales factory.

Performance Analysis

Ski Units Completed:	*Week 1*	*Week 2*	*Week 3*	*Week 4*
South Wales	1,200	1,350	1,400	1,300
Yorkshire	1,000	1,050	1,150	1,100
Budgeted labour hours per ski unit				
(the same for each factory)				
Moulding	3.4			
Assembly	4.3			
Finishing	6.4			
Actual hours worked	*Week 1*	*Week 2*	*Week 3*	*Week 4*
South Wales:				
Moulding	4,200	4,320	4,760	4,940
Assembly	4,950	5,795	5,995	5,724
Finishing	7,432	8,745	9,315	8,562
Yorkshire:				
Moulding	3,600	3,570	4,025	3,810
Assembly	4,213	4,530	5,120	4,875
Finishing	6,457	7,021	7,765	6,912

Standard hours produced

(Ski units completed × budgeted hours per ski unit)

South Wales:

Moulding	4,080	4,590	4,760	4,420
Assembly	5,160	5,805	6,020	5,590
Finishing	7,680	8,640	8,960	8,320

Yorkshire:

Moulding	3,400	3,570	3,910	3,740
Assembly	4,300	4,515	4,945	4,730
Finishing	6,400	6,720	7,360	7,040

Variance (hours worked)

South Wales:

Moulding	(120)	270	0	(520)
Assembly	210	10	25	(134)
Finishing	248	(105)	(355)	(242)
Total	338	175	(330)	(896)

Yorkshire:

Moulding	(200)	0	(115)	(70)
Assembly	87	(15)	(175)	(145)
Finishing	(57)	(301)	(405)	128
Total	(170)	(316)	(695)	(87)

Required

(a)   Calculate the total actual hours worked in each factory and the actual hours per ski unit produced (to one decimal place). Present your results in the table below.

	Week 1	Week 2	Week 3	Week 4
Total Actual Hours				
South Wales				
Yorkshire				
Ski Units Completed				
South Wales	1,200	1,350	1,400	1,300
Yorkshire	1,000	1,050	1,150	1,100
Hours per Unit				
South Wales				
Yorkshire				

(b)   Write a report for Mr O'Hagan which compares the efficiency of the two factories and highlights any problem areas. The report should also consider the limitations of the analysis carried out and possible reasons for the differences in performance.

4 Resource utilisation

4.1 Introduction

Definition   **Resource utilisation** is a measure of the extent to which resources were used in relation to resources available.

4.2 Manufacturing operations

Machine and labour utilisation can be measured as hours spent in production (productive hours) to hours available (ie machine capacity or labour hours paid).

4.3 Example: resource utilisation in manufacturing

A printing machine has the capacity to print 5,000 A4 pages per hour. During one 40-hour week, 120,000 pages were printed. The labour force spent 140 hours that week working on products although 160 hours were paid for. Calculate the machine and labour utilisation.

4.4 Solution

The machine must have been used for 120,000/5,000 = 24 hours in the week. Thus the machine utilisation in the week was $24/40$ = 60%. (This could equally well be measured as 120,000/(5,000 × 40)).

Labour utilisation $140/160$ = 87.5%.

The low labour utilisation is probably due to idle time.

4.5 Non-manufacturing operations

Examples of suitable utilisation measures for various types of **service activities** are as follows:

Professional   Chargeable hours: total hours paid

Public transport   Passenger miles: total miles run

Hotel   Rooms occupied: rooms available (occupancy rate)

5 Profitability

5.1 Introduction

The profitability of an organisation can be assessed by looking at the gross profit margin, net profit margin and return on capital employed.

These figures will be illustrated in the following example using the figures given below for GJ Ltd.

Summarised balance sheet at 31 December 20X1

	£000	£000
Fixed assets		2,600
Current assets		
Stocks	600	
Debtors	900	
Cash at bank and in hand	100	
	1,600	
Current liabilities	800	
		800
Capital employed		3,400

Summarised profit and loss account for the year ended 31 December 20X1

	£000
Sales	6,000
Cost of sales	4,000
Gross profit	2,000
Administrative expenses	(1,506)
Distribution and marketing	(74)
Net profit before interest and tax	420

5.2   Return on capital employed (ROCE)

Capital employed represents the long-term investment in the business by the **owners** in the form of **equity** (sole trader, partners or shareholders) and **other investors** in the form of **debt** (eg providers of long-term loans). In the case of GJ Ltd, there being no long-term loans, capital employed is just represented by owners' capital and is equivalent to net assets.

Return on capital employed is frequently regarded as the best measure of profitability, indicating how successful a business is in utilising its assets. There are a number of ways that ROCE may be calculated; the basic formula is as follows:

$$\text{ROCE} = \frac{\text{Net profit before interest and tax}}{\text{Capital employed}} \times 100$$

5.3   Example

What is the return on capital employed for GJ Ltd?

5.4   Solution

$$\text{ROCE} = \frac{420}{3,400} \times 100 = 12.35\%$$

5.5 Return on equity

Return on equity (RoE) measure the profitability of the non-debt investment in the business. It would be expressed simply as:

$$RoE = \frac{\text{Net profit after interest}}{\text{Equity}} \times 100$$

It is important to ensure that you use the correct combination of profit and capital employed:

- profit before interest – can be combined with all capital (equity + debt)

- profit after interest – can be combined with equity alone

5.6 Example

A business has profit before interest of £160,000 and an interest charge of £20,000. The capital of the business is made up of a long term loan of £200,000 and equity funds of £1,000,000.

What is the return on capital employed and the return on equity for the business?

5.7 Solution

$$ROCE = \frac{\text{Profit before interest}}{\text{Equity} + \text{debt}} \times 100$$

$$= \frac{160,000}{1,200,000} \times 100$$

$$= 13.3\%$$

$$RoE = \frac{\text{Profit after interest}}{\text{Equity}} \times 100$$

$$= \frac{160,000 - 20,000}{1,000,000} \times 100$$

$$= 14\%$$

5.8 Net profit margin (on sales)

A **low margin** indicates low selling prices or high costs or both. Comparative analysis will reveal the level of prices and costs in relation to competitors.

$$NPM = \frac{\text{Net profit}}{\text{Sales}} \times 100$$

5.9 Example

What is the net profit margin for GJ Ltd?

5.10 Solution

$$NPM = \frac{420}{6,000} \times 100 = 7.0\%$$

5.11   Gross profit margin

The gross profit margin isolates the pure 'nuts and bolts' of a business, ie ignoring indirect expenses and sundry income. It considers the profitability of the actual production or trading element of the business.

$$\text{GPM} \ = \ \frac{\text{Gross profit}}{\text{Sales}} \times 100$$

5.12   Example

What is the gross profit margin for GJ Ltd?

5.13   Solution

$$\text{GPM} = \frac{2,000}{6,000} \times 100 = 33\tfrac{1}{3}\%$$

5.14   Breakdown of ROCE

Return on capital employed is made up of two figures – the net profit margin and asset turnover:

$$\text{ROCE} = \text{net profit margin} \times \text{asset turnover}$$

So in any analysis of return on capital employed it is worth breaking down the ratio into these two component parts and analysing each separately.

5.15   Asset turnover

Asset turnover could be described as a measure of resource utilisation and is sometimes called capital productivity. It is a measure of how much turnover or sales is being earned by each £ of capital employed and is calculated as:

$$\text{Asset turnover} = \frac{\text{Sales}}{\text{Capital employed}}$$

5.16   Example

What is the asset turnover for GJ Ltd?

Show how the ROCE is made up of asset turnover and net profit margin.

5.17   Solution

$$\text{Asset turnover} \ = \ \frac{6,000}{3,400}$$

$$= \ 1.76$$

This indicates that every £1 of capital employed by GJ Ltd is earning £1.76 of turnover. It is a measure of how hard the assets of the business are being worked.

$$\text{ROCE} \ = \ \text{asset turnover} \times \text{net profit margin}$$

$$= \ 1.76 \times 7\% = 12.35\%$$

6 Interpretation of ratios

6.1 Introduction

We shall now look at why **care needs to be taken in interpreting ratios.**

First a couple of general points to bear in mind when looking at a set of accounts with a view to commenting on the position they indicate:

- Before you start calculating ratios, **read the accounts** to identify any obvious points. You do not need a ratio to tell you that sales levels have doubled, for example.

- **Try to look at ratios in groups** rather than in isolation; a group of ratios may provide a clearer indication of where the cause lies. Group together the ROCE, net and gross profit margins and asset turnover to try to get a picture of what is happening in the business.

6.2 Inter-firm comparison of ROCE

As we have seen, the aim of the ROCE is to see how effectively the business is using the money invested in it. This can be compared to a target figure or to ROCE for earlier periods.

It may be valid to compare this ratio with that of our rivals, but some care needs to be taken here.

6.3 Example

Z Ltd, a recently formed company, has ROCE of $\dfrac{£5,000}{£50,000}$ = 10%.

Z Ltd's main rival is A Ltd, a long-established company. The two companies are identical except that A Ltd has capital employed of only £40,000. Compare the ROCE of the two companies.

6.4 Solution

A Ltd's ROCE is $\dfrac{5,000}{40,000}$ = 12.5%.

Clearly, the two different figures for ROCE do not imply that A Ltd is necessarily a better company than Z Ltd.

- Be aware of the **age structure of companies' capital** before comparing them. A Ltd's fixed assets will be older and having been depreciated longer will have a lower net book value therefore a lower capital employed.

- Often **new investment does not bring immediate profits.** This may be for a number of reasons. It may take time for the company's employees to learn to use the new equipment. Alternatively, it may take the company time to obtain enough orders to use the new facilities to the full. (This may result in a temporary reduction in the ROCE.)

6.5 Interpretation of gross and net profit margins

By looking at these two ratios together, we can determine whether a change in the net profit margin can be explained by deteriorating trade success or other expense charges.

6.6   *Example*

	20X1	20X0
	£000	£000
Sales	100	100
Cost of sales	82	80
Gross profit	18	20
Overheads	11	10
Net profit	7	10

Compare the gross and net profit margins of the business for the two years.

6.7   *Solution*

	20X1	20X0
GPM	18%	20%
NPM	7%	10%

The net profit margin has fallen fairly dramatically this year. This can partly be explained by a decrease in gross profit margin but also by an increase in overheads.

This is an illustration of using more than one ratio to guide our thoughts.

Activity 3 (The answer is in the final chapter of this book)

Business Computers Ltd

Data

Business Computers Ltd is a computer company specialising in the manufacture of hardware, software and the provision of related consultancy services. The company is split into three divisions:

> Hardware – Commercial
>
> Hardware – Government
>
> Software services and consultancy services

The company has traditionally traded in the hardware market, selling computers to business and government organisations. However, in recent years an increasing amount of business is being done in software services for the company's own products and related consultancy provision.

The company is now reviewing its products, services and markets. The commercial hardware market is likely to become more competitive with development costs rising. The government hardware market will be restricted by government spending limits over the next three years. However, the long–term projection is that more government departments and organisations will adopt more commercial practices and demand products the company produces. The software services and consultancy division work originated from government contracts and most of the company's work comes from this source.

You work in the finance department of the company as an Accounting Technician and you have been given a number of tasks by the Financial Accountant in order to provide information for the review.

Results for the 20X4/X5 financial years were as follows.

Year			Hardware – Commercial	Hardware – Government	Software & Consultancy
			£	£	£
20X5	Sales		15,957,000	24,768,000	11,368,000
20X5	Development costs		6,376,000	7,832,000	2,134,000
20X5	Other costs		7,215,000	8,150,000	3,716,000
20X5	Number of employees		831	607	423
20X4	Sales		17,643,000	25,974,000	9,276,000

Note. It is company policy to write off development costs in the year of expenditure because of the pace of technological change within the industry.

Task 1

Complete the following table of ratios for 20X5. The ratios for 20X4 are given.

Business Computers Limited

Table of ratios

Division	Ratio	20X4	20X5
Hardware – Commercial	Net profit/sales	17.5%	
	Development costs/sales	34.7%	
	Sales per employee	£22,107	
Hardware – Government	Net profit/sales	36.6%	
	Development costs/sales	30.9%	
	Sales per employee	£41,200	
Software & Consultancy	Net profit/sales	39.4%	
	Development costs/sales	21.7%	
	Sales per employee	£23,614	

Task 2

Write a detailed report to the financial accountant using the report format below, comparing divisional performance between 20X4 and 20X5 and giving recommendations for the company's future division.

BUSINESS COMPUTERS LTD

REPORT ON DIVISIONAL PERFORMANCE

To:

From:

Date:

7   *Analysis of results by organisational unit*

7.1   **Introduction**

Whilst most outside users of financial accounts will be concerned only with the performance of the organisation as a whole, this will not generally give useful information to the **managers** of the organisation, unless it is a small, one product/service business.

Many organisations will therefore generate additional information from their accounting and administrative systems that breaks down the **overall revenues and costs between the organisational units** within the business, as defined by management.

7.2   *Organisational units*

The term **organisational units** is used here to cover all of the following:

♦   divisions

♦   departments (productive and service/support)

♦   sales areas

♦   processes

♦   products/services

Not all organisations will require separate information for each of these. Relevant divisions and/or departments will be closely linked with the organisational structure, as discussed in the first chapter.

 Management will need to know how these units are performing individually as part of the responsibility accounting system – **unit managers being held responsible** for revenues and costs under their control attributable to their unit.

Even if there are no separately operating divisions or departments, a business that has **more than one type of output** (different products or services) will inevitably wish to assess the separate costs/profitability of these.

 For Unit 7 you need to be able to carry out simple analyses of given revenue and/or cost figures between divisions, products, etc. and to assess the results. Once the results are split, much of the performance appraisal process will be exactly as discussed earlier in this chapter.

7.3   *Divisions and departments*

The divisions or departments within an organisation will often be accounted for as **profit centres** – that is, both revenues and costs can be traced to them, allowing the calculation of an individual profit figure for each centre.

Examples of divisionalised/departmentalised businesses include the following:

♦   Organisations operating through **branches** (banks, travel and estate agents, retail shops/stores, etc)

♦   Organisations operating on a **regional basis** (utilities, health authorities, manufacturers/wholesalers, etc)

♦   Organisations split into **separate departments within the same location** (department stores, accountants/solicitors firms, local authorities, etc)

All of these types of individual units will be centrally controlled via a **head office** or central board.

With careful use, these individual profit figures can be analysed in order to allow assessment of the performance of both the division/department itself and the **manager responsible for it**. There will generally be departmental targets set for this purpose.

The separate results will be combined or **consolidated** within the overall financial/ management accounts for the organisation as a whole.

7.4   Problem areas

In setting up **accounting and performance appraisal systems** for separate divisions/departments, consideration must be made of the best method for dealing with the following aspects:

- shared costs (overheads)

- head office costs

- traceable/controllable costs

- transactions between departments/divisions

- consolidation of results

7.5   Shared costs

In many departmentalised businesses, costs will be incurred that relate to **more than one department**, for example:

- buildings costs where a building is occupied by more than one department

- shared support/service departments (eg maintenance, canteen, accounts)

- advertising and marketing costs

Each department should generally be held responsible for a **share of these costs,** on the basis that, if the department did not exist, the level of costs incurred would generally be lowered.

An appropriate basis for **apportioning** each shared cost between the departments needs to be established.

Shared cost	*Basis for apportionment*
Buildings costs (rent, rates, heat/light, etc)	Floor area
Maintenance	Maintenance hours
Canteen	Number of employees
Accounts	Volume of transactions
Advertising and marketing	Revenue

The process of allocation and apportionment of such costs is principally assessable in Unit 6.

7.6   Head office costs

The **head office,** or other **central management unit** for a departmentalised/divisionalised business will incur its own costs – management salaries, administrative costs, premises costs, etc. Unless these costs can be identified with the organisational units in a meaningful way, resulting divisional net profit figures can be misleading in assessing performance.

 It is therefore usual to **omit head office costs** from individual units' results analyses, including them as a total figure only when consolidating the results for the overall accounts.

7.7 Traceable/controllable costs

In assessing the results of a department/division, all revenues and costs that are **traceable to that unit** will generally be included.

 **Definition** **Traceable costs** or controllable costs are those costs which are incurred as a result of the department/division being in operation.

For example, this will include wages and salaries of the unit's employees, variable costs of production/service and other overheads (variable and fixed) that relate directly to the unit. This may include apportioned costs, if the basis used gives a fair indication of the cost that would be saved if the unit were to close.

 To assess the manager of the unit, however, only the traceable costs that are **controllable** by him/her should be included in the profit figure used to assess performance.

Thus, although the **manager's salary** is traceable to the unit, the manager is unlikely to have control over its level! Additionally, the depreciation and other **costs of fixed assets** that were acquired through head-office decisions should be excluded from managerial assessment.

7.8 Example

A summary divisional report might appear as follows:

	Division X £000	*Division Y* £000	*Total* £000
Controllable elements			
Sales	820	510	1,330
Variable costs	(460)	(340)	(800)
Contribution	360	170	530
Fixed costs	(125)	(54)	(179)
Controllable profit	235	116	351
Other traceable costs (including apportioned costs)	(240)	(72)	(312)
Traceable profit/(loss)	(5)	44	39
Head office costs			(12)
Profit			27
Contribution/sales (%)	43.9%	33.3%	39.8%
Controllable profit margin	28.7%	22.7%	26.4%
Traceable profit/(loss) margin	(0.6%)	8.6%	2.9%

Comment on the position shown by this divisional report.

7.9 Solution

The **controllable contribution and profit lines** should be used in the **assessment of the managers**. Division X's contribution margin is considerably better than that of Division Y, although this advantage is lessened at the controllable profit level. Division X's manager perhaps needs to review his fixed costs to ensure they are all necessary and being properly controlled (although the two divisions' cost structures may be expected to be different if they are concerned with different lines of business).

The **contribution line** may also be used in the **assessment of the division**, as it is likely to be the traceable as well as controllable contribution; most variable costs will be under the control of the manager. Both divisions have a generally healthy operational performance, ie on a short-term basis.

However, the **traceable profit/(loss) line** indicates that Division X does not appear to have a longer-term future, unless fixed costs can be reduced. The validity of this conclusion will depend upon the proportion of traceable fixed costs that are apportioned and the extent to which this apportionment reflects the true use of the resources by the divisions and thus the costs that may be saved if the division were to close.

7.10 Transactions between departments/divisions

In some departmentalised/divisionalised organisations, **units will use each other's products or services**.

For example, a manufacturer's production process may be split between machining, assembly and packing units and products are passed from one unit to another; a tuition college may have a printing department which is used by the publishing and courses department, etc.

How should such transactions be accounted for in a divisional/departmental accounting system? This will depend to a certain extent upon the **degree of autonomy of the units**. Possibilities include the following:

♦ One unit may be treated as a **'subsidiary'** of another, as in a cost centre being part of a profit centre. In this case, all the costs of the cost centre will be charged to the profit centre as with any other cost. An example would be an alterations department within a clothing department of a shop/store.

♦ If the cost centre provides goods/services to more than one profit centre (as in the printing department of the tuition college), the costs of that department could be **split between the profit centres** using a basis that reflects the degree of usage by each profit centre (as in the allocation and apportionment of costs of a service department).

♦ Thus the printing department's costs may be split between publishing and courses according to the volume of work carried out for each.

♦ If all units involved are to be treated as profit centres, then some form of charge for goods/services provided from one unit to another will need to be recorded in each unit's accounts. Such a charge would be known as a **transfer price**.

7.11 Setting a transfer price

Possible **bases for setting a transfer price** are as follows.

(i)   **Actual cost**: If goods/services were transferred at actual cost (marginal or full), the supplying unit will not record a profit as such. It will also provide no incentive for cost control.

(ii)   **Standard cost**: This will help to contain cost variances within the responsible unit and will encourage cost control.

(iii)   **Cost plus**: Transfers recorded at cost plus an allowance for contribution/profit will share the final profit between the contributing units.

(iv)   **Market price**: If the supplying unit could sell its output to other organisations as well as to units within its own, the transfer price may be based upon the outside market price. Adjustments may be made to allow for differences in packaging/distribution costs, credit terms, etc.

Each unit will then be assessed upon revenues and costs that are commercially based, ie that imitate the situation if each unit were selling/buying to/from the outside market. This will generally promote decisions re output levels, etc. that are optimum for the organisation as a whole.

7.12   Consolidation of results

When **consolidating the results** from different operating units to give an overall result for the organisation, care must be taken to ensure that the figures have been prepared on a **comparable basis**. Problems in this respect will arise mainly in combining divisions that are largely operated independently of each other, with managers given a high degree of responsibility. Examples of the sort of problems that may arise include the following:

♦   costs being categorised differently

♦   different accounting policies being used (eg for depreciation, stock, research and development expenditure, etc.)

♦   differing attitudes being used in determining the level of bad debt provision, stock write-downs, etc.

♦   inter-departmental transfers being recorded at different amounts in the books of the units involved

These problems can largely be overcome by **setting up standard organisational policies and procedures**, but this will remove a degree of the autonomy of the units.

If the individual units are to be allowed some freedom in deciding policies, etc. there will need to be a **reconciliation exercise** carried out at head office to bring the results in line with each other for consolidation.

7.13   Transfers between divisions

As we have seen it is often the case in a divisionalised organisation that there will be transfers of goods or services between divisions and these will be charged to the receiving division at a transfer price.

This means that this transfer price will be included in the 'selling' division's sales figure and in the 'purchasing' division's cost of sales. When consolidating the divisions' performance these transfers must be excluded in order to give a true figure for the sales to external organisations and purchases from external organisations.

7.14 Example

A business has two divisions with the following summarised results for the last month:

	Division A £	Division B £
Sales	108,000	155,000
Cost of sales	63,000	89,000
	45,000	66,000
Less: expenses	23,000	34,000
Net profit	22,000	32,000

During the month Division B transferred goods to Division A at a transfer price of £16,000.

Prepare the consolidated results for the month.

7.15 Solution

	Division A £	Division B £	Adjustments	Total
Sales	108,000	155,000	(16,000)	247,000
Cost of sales	63,000	89,000	(16,000)	136,000
	45,000	66,000		111,000
Less: expenses	23,000	34,000		57,000
Net profit	22,000	32,000		54,000

The interdivisional sale must be excluded from both sales and cost of sales as it has been recorded as a sale in Division B's books and as a purchase in Division A's books.

Activity 4 *(The answer is in the final chapter of this book)*

Grand Hotel Group

Your company, the Grand Hotel Group, operates a chain of three hotels in Southern England. The group has been affected in recent years by the recession. The management of the group have been rather worried by the recent downturn in profitability and called in a firm of management consultants in mid 20X1.

As a result of the review by the management consultants, a programme was undertaken to restore profitability. This included the following actions:

(1) A reduction in the number of part-time staff with remaining staff put on a full-time basis

(2) A planned reduction in fixed charges (ie administrative expenses, rent, rates, etc.)

(3) An organised marketing campaign to increase revenue from weekend and mid-week bargain breaks and conferences. The campaign was to emphasise the competitive pricing of such services and the campaign costs are included in other variable operating expenses.

The programme was implemented in the Autumn of 20X1 and the first results of it are shown in the 20X2 accounts. A summary of the accounts is given on the following page.

You have been asked by the hotel management to evaluate the success of the programme put forward by the management consultants' review.

Assume the hotels are open for 365 days each year and work to the nearest £.

Assessment tasks

Task 1

Calculate for 20X0, 20X1 and 20X2:

(a)   net profit

(b)   net profit as a percentage of turnover

(c)   average staff costs

(d)   turnover at year 1 (20X0) prices

Write a short report highlighting any significant trends and drawing management's attention to items you consider worthy of consideration.

Task 2

(a)   Calculate four different ratios for 20X0, 20X1 and 20X2 to evaluate the effectiveness of the programme implemented as a result of the management consultant's review summarising your findings in the form of a short report.

(b)   What further information would help you to quantify the success of the programme introduced by the group?

The Grand Hotel Group

	20X0 £	20X1 £	20X2 £
Turnover	3,200,000	2,910,000	3,600,000
Costs			
Food and beverages	240,000	220,000	400,000
Payroll and related expenses	720,000	680,000	660,000
Other variable operating expenses	220,000	200,000	380,000
Fixed charges (admin. expenses, rent, rates, etc.)	1,800,000	1,800,000	1,700,000
Other information			
Number of employees (full-time equivalents)	140	130	115
Number of rooms	120	120	120
Number of rooms let	28,400	26,400	35,300
Retail Price Index	100	107	111
UK unemployment	5.3%	6.8%	9.2%
Average household disposable income	£19,050	£18,750	£18,250

Activity 5 *(The answer is in the final chapter of this book)*

BTC

Until three years ago, BTC, an accountancy training organisation, ran its own fleet of vans and delivered manuals to retailers and colleges. The decision was taken to concentrate on core activities and so several organisations were carefully considered before RD plc was selected to take on the responsibility for storing and delivering the manuals. It was agreed that RD would purchase the manuals from BTC at the recommended selling price, less an agreed discount. This ensures that RD would automatically benefit from future increases in the selling price of the manuals. The arrangement has worked well for both organisations and a good relationship has been established.

The managing director of RD has been satisfied with the profits that have been earned, but he is concerned with the efficiency of the transport operation. You, as the assistant accountant, have been asked to provide regular information to the general manager, who is responsible for all aspects of transportation. The general manager has always controlled this area by observing what he calls 'key ratios' which he sees as delivery costs and drivers' wages as a percentage of sales, sales per van and the number of deliveries. He believes that, if these ratios are improving, then the transport operation is working well. He is also a great believer that graphs help to clarify the statistics in any report.

Appendix 1

Years	1	2	3
Sales (£)	200,000	222,200	272,630
Van expenses (£)	14,000	15,000	18,000
As percentage of sales (%)	7	6.7	6.6
Drivers' wages (£)	52,000	56,600	68,150
As percentage of sales (%)	26	25.5	25
Number of vans	3	3	4
Sales per van (£)	66,667	74,067	68,158
Number of deliveries	1,000	1,100	1,400
Sales per delivery (£)	200	202	195

The accountant, although very interested in performance measures, is worried about the information in Appendix 1. His main concern is that the selling prices of the manuals have increased dramatically over the last two years. This was due to BTC's policy of initially pricing below the normal market price and then, once the manuals had been accepted by the market, increasing prices quite sharply. The accountant wants to remove these specific price rises from the figures before calculating the 'key ratios' and has produced the following index numbers of price changes based on Year 1.

Years	1	2	3
Sales	100	110	137
Van expenses	100	104	106

Drivers' wages have shown very little change during these years and can remain as per Appendix 1.

Task 1

Complete Appendix 2 below by:

(a)   Converting the actual figures for Years 2 and 3 (from Appendix 1) to Year 1 prices by using the price index given (calculations to the nearest £).

(b)   Calculating the 'key ratios' including sales per delivery £s (calculations to one decimal place).

Appendix 2

Years	1	2	3
Sales (£)	200,000		
Van expenses (£)	14,000		
As percentage of sales	7		
Drivers' wages (£)	52,000	56,600	68,150
As percentage of sales	26		
Number of vans	3	3	4
Sales per van (£)	66,667		
Number of deliveries	1,000	1,100	1,400
Sales per delivery (£)	200		

Task 2

Write a report to the general manager commenting upon the performance of the transport operation. The report should be in three sections.

Section 1:   should explain whether the 'key ratios' in Appendix 1 support the general manager's opinion

Section 2:   should explain whether the 'key ratios' in Appendix 2 indicate an efficient operation

Section 3:   (a)   should state whether you consider that the transport operation is efficient and whether Appendix 1 or Appendix 2 should be the basis of future reports, giving reasons for your decisions

                 (b)   should also suggest one other 'key ratio' that should be observed (no calculation is required) and say how often this type of information should be presented

8   Summary

This chapter has covered all areas of internal reporting for organisational units. We started by looking at performance indicators covering cost per unit, productivity, resource utilisation and profitability. In particular we considered gross and net profit margins, return on capital employed and asset turnover and how these are all related.

The performance indicators considered can be calculated for an organisation as a whole or for separate areas or divisions of an organisation. If an organisation is divisionalised then this will provide further problems to consider. The assessment of a divisional manager's performance must be carefully assessed excluding head office costs and non-traceable or controllable costs.

A final problem that was considered was the issue of transactions between divisions. If a transfer price is charged by one division providing goods or services to another then when the divisional results are consolidated the amount of the goods transferred in the period must be deducted from both sales and cost of sales.

CHAPTER 6

Reporting to external agencies

ASSESSMENT FOCUS

Assessments may include a requirement to complete a form or report to an external agency. This will normally require calculation of the types of performance indicators considered in the previous chapter and will normally consist of filling in a form with the relevant details.

This chapter covers the following Knowledge and Understanding and Performance Criteria of the AAT Syllabus.

> Relevant information is identified, collated and presented in accordance with the conventions and definitions used by outside agencies (*Performance Criteria element 7.2*)

> Calculations of ratios and performance indicators are accurate (*Performance Criteria element 7.2*)

> Authorisation for the despatch of the completed reports and returns is sought from the appropriate person (*Performance Criteria element 7.2*)

> Reports and returns are presented in accordance with outside agencies' requirements and deadlines (*Performance Criteria element 7.2*)

> Main types of outside organisations requiring reports and returns: regulatory; grant awarding; information collecting; trade associations (*Knowledge and Understanding element 7.2*)

> Main types of performance indicators: productivity; cost per unit; resource utilisation; profitability (*Knowledge and Understanding elements 7.1, 7.2*)

> Ratios: gross profit margin; net profit margin; return on capital employed (*Knowledge and Understanding element 7.1, 7.2*)

> Background understanding that a variety of outside agencies may require reports and returns from organisations and that these requirements must be built into administrative and accounting systems and procedures (*Knowledge and Understanding element 7.2, 7.3*)

In order to cover these the following topics are included.

> The types of external agencies likely to require a report or return
> How to complete standard forms
> The importance of accuracy in external reports and returns
> The importance of authorisation of a complete report or return before it is despatched

1 *External agencies requiring reports and returns*

1.1 Introduction

The second element of Unit 7 concerns the preparation of reports and returns for external agencies. The main types of external parties that may require a report or return from an organisation are considered below.

1.2 Regulatory organisations

There are a number of regulatory organisations which will require regular and non-regular reports and returns. These include:

♦ The Inland Revenue – on a regular basis organisations must send details of their employees' payroll details to the Inland Revenue detailing the Income Tax (PAYE) and National Insurance Contributions deducted from employees' gross pay

Companies must also provide annual corporation tax returns

♦ HM Customs and Excise – the VAT return (covered in detail in a later chapter)

♦ Department of Trade and Industry – companies must produce annual financial statements

♦ Health and Safety Executive, Training Commission, Local Authorities' Planning Departments – these government agencies often require non-financial information regarding the operations, employment policies and plans of the business

♦ Sector regulatory bodies – for example financial services organisations, banks and listed companies are required to submit regular returns concerning their operations and financial position to the appropriate regulatory body such as the FSA, The Bank of England and the Stock Exchange.

1.3 Grant awarding organisations

There are a variety of both government and privately funded schemes which make various awards and grants available to businesses. An example is the Enterprise Initiative Scheme run by the DTI to offer grants, information and advisory services to businesses.

In order to support any application for a grant the business will need to provide a range of both financial and non-financial information, including details of recent performance and profitability, details of the purpose to which the grant will be put, current and future employee details ie is the grant award due to provide opportunities for additional employment?

1.4 Information collecting organisations

There are a number of agencies which collect information from businesses for analysis for their own purposes and for use by other interested parties, often including the organisations supplying the information.

Examples include:

♦ Office for National Statistics collects information for the compilation of reports and statistics on business performance, consumer expenditure patterns and social trends.

♦ General market survey organisations – the information required from such organisations is of course voluntary and you should ensure that you only ever provide such information if it is the policy of your organisation to do so.

1.5 Trade associations

Definition   Trade associations are bodies that represent and look after the interests of organisations in the same line of business such as the Publishers' Association or the Association of British Travel Agents (ABTA).

Trade associations conduct voluntary surveys of member businesses concerning such things as wage rates, employment practices, debtor levels, stock holding patterns, fixed asset utilisation and many others. This information is collated and is often put together in the form of an **inter-**

firm comparison for this type of business. This inter-firm comparison is then provided to members in order that they can assess their own stock levels, debtor levels etc against the average, highest and lowest in their sector.

When providing information to trade associations it is likely that this will be required in the form of key ratios such as gross profit and net profit margins and return on capital employed. The trade association may also require information on cost per unit, productivity and resource utilisation. As well as this financial information the trade association may also require non-financial information regarding employment policies, customer profiles etc.

1.6 Nature of information required for external reports

Most of the information required for external reports and returns will be in the form of performance indicators as covered in the previous chapter. There may also be some absolute figures required such as the year end debtor or creditor totals which can be found from the year end financial statements.

1.7 Problems of reporting for external agencies

As we have seen much of the information required for external reports and returns will be available from the normal accounting and administrative systems of the organisation, such as VAT, PAYE and NIC details. However some of the information required is specialised, such as financial statistics and non-financial data which may or may not be part of the organisation's own management accounting requirements.

Therefore there may be a need to set up special data collecting exercises or routines in order to pick up the relevant data and sort it as required for the particular report or return.

 Reporting to an external agency may require information that is not normally part of the management information of the organisation.

2 Standard forms

2.1 Introduction

Most of the returns that you will have to fill out for external agencies will be on pre-printed standard forms. This will make it more likely that the external agency will get the precise information that it requires in the correct format and that information provided by different organisations will be directly comparable.

2.2 Why use forms?

 Forms can be a very efficient means by which routine data can be collected or information conveyed. Properly constructed forms will ensure that the **relevant** information at the **right level of detail** in the **required format** is given to the user.

They will generally be relatively **quick and easy to complete,** and are more likely to encourage **prompt submission** of the required information than if a fully written report were requested.

2.3 Principles of good form design

The qualities of a well-constructed form are outlined below. If you are aware of these it will help you when completing pre-printed forms.

2.4   Requirements

Requirements must be clearly explained and unambiguous

◆ Terminology must be **standardised** and explained on the back of the form if necessary.

◆ The **order of completion** of the form (if it matters) should be logical and clear.

◆ If **calculations** are required, they should be clearly explained. For example, if the calculation is to multiply or sum the contents of two boxes on the form, these should be numbered or lettered and the required calculation indicated using the numbers or letters.

◆ If figures are to be given to a **particular level of accuracy** (say to the nearest £), this should be clearly indicated.

2.5   Contents

The amount of writing required should be minimised

◆ As much information as possible should be **pre-printed**.

◆ The use of **boxes to tick** or a choice of possible answers offered will cut down on the writing.

2.6   Destination

The destination of the completed form(s) should be clearly indicated

◆ A section indicating the **name and department or address** of the department or person to whom the form should be returned should be included on the form rather than on a separate accompanying letter or in a manual.

◆ If the form is multi-part, the **destination of each part** should be clearly shown.

2.7   Form-filling

When **completing a form**, either as part of your assessment, or in practice, you should remember the following points:

◆ Have a **quick look through the whole form first**, to ascertain what information will be required for its completion. It will also help to avoid information being given in the wrong place on the form.

◆ Ensure you **follow general instructions** regarding the method of completion (eg. in pen, block capitals, figures to two decimal places, option numbers to be crossed through or circled etc.).

◆ Keep **written responses as concise as possible**, preferably within the space provided. However, you should re-read the requirement to ensure you have answered all parts. For example, on a form for a theft insurance claim, you may be asked to explain the circumstances in which the theft took place 'including the exact location of the property at the time, the estimated time of theft, the mode of access and the nature of any security measures taken'.

◆ Ensure you have **completed all parts of the form**.

As part of an assessment you are likely to have to complete a form for an external agency. This is largely a matter of common sense and following instructions.

Activity 1 *(The answer is in the final chapter of this book)*

NTL plc

The Toy Manufacturer's Trade Association was established several years ago to assist its member companies with legal/administrative matters and to provide an advisory service. You are employed by the Trade Association and are mainly involved with the advisory service. One of the services offered is an inter-firm comparison which involves collecting quarterly information from its member companies. After analysis, the best and average results are supplied to all participating firms but no company names are revealed. It is up to each company to compare their own results with the figures provided and to decide what action needs to be taken. NTL plc, a new company to this service, asks for your help as it does not understand what calculations it needs to do or what conclusions to draw. The most recent figures for NTL plc are as follows:

Trading and profit and loss a/c for quarter to 30 September 20X3

	£	£
Sales		653,000
Materials	361,109	
Labour	80,319	
Production overheads	108,398	
Production cost		549,826
Distribution and marketing		18,937
Administration		44,404
Total cost		613,167
Net profit		39,833

Balance sheet as at 30 September 20X3

	£	£
Fixed assets		185,729
Current assets		
Stock	92,046	
Debtors	56,192	
	148,238	
Current liabilities		
Creditors	48,075	
Overdraft	40,009	
	88,084	
Working capital		60,154
Capital employed		245,883

Assessment tasks

Task 1

Complete the form below by calculating the inter-firm ratios for NTL plc (calculations to one decimal place).

Toy Manufacturer's Trade Association

Inter-firm comparison report, Quarter to 30 September 20X3

	Most profitable	*Average*	*NTL plc*
Direct materials as a percentage of sales	46.9	52.6	
Direct labour as a percentage of sales	10.4	10.1	
Production overheads as a percentage of sales	14.0	16.9	
Production cost as a percentage of sales	71.3	79.6	
Distribution and marketing as a percentage of sales	4.9	3.8	
Administration as a percentage of sales	5.6	5.7	
Net profit as a percentage of sales	18.2	10.9	
Net profit as a percentage of capital employed	40.4	22.6	
Current ratio (current assets to current liabilities)	2.2 to 1	1.9 to 1	
Quick ratio (debtors to current liabilities)	1.1 to 1	0.9 to 1	

Task 2

Write a report to the managing director of NTL plc explaining the main differences revealed in Task 1. Comment on both the profitability and the financial position of the company, suggesting areas for further investigation and possible corrective action.

Task 3

The managing director is under pressure from the other managers to spend £20,000 on an advertising campaign, which it is believed would increase sales by 10%. An investigation into production overheads has shown that £32,658 was variable and £75,740 was fixed. To test out the proposed advertising campaign you are asked to:

(a)   Recalculate the trading and profit and loss account to 30 September 20X3. Assume that material, labour and variable production overheads increase at the same rate as sales (calculations to the nearest £). (A blank form is given below.)

Re-worked trading and profit and loss account for quarter to 30 September 20X3

£

Sales

_____

Materials
Labour
Variable production overheads
Fixed production overheads
Production cost
Distribution and marketing (fixed)
Advertising campaign (fixed)
Administration (fixed)

_____

Total cost

_____

Net profit

_____

(b)   Write a brief report to the managing director explaining whether or not the advertising campaign is justified.

3   Accuracy and authority

3.1   Introduction

When preparing a report to an external agency you will be providing someone outside the organisation with important information about your own organisation.   Therefore it is extremely important that all information is accurate and that the report or return is authorised before being sent out.

3.2   Accuracy

When completing a return or report it is essential that the information required is accurate.

♦   If there are any instructions or formulae given for calculation or performance indicators ensure that you use precisely the figures that are requested.

♦   Check that you have picked out the correct figures from your organisation's data, for example if asked for the balance of debtors at 30 June 20X0 you should not be providing the debtors' balance at 31 July 20X0.

♦   Check and double check all calculations that you have made on the report or return.

3.3   Deadlines

Ensure that the report or return is completed, ready for authorisation well before the stated deadline for the report or return. This is particularly important for returns to regulatory bodies such as the Inland Revenue or HM Customs and Excise as a late return can result in a fine for the organisation.

3.4   Authorisation

No report or return should ever be sent out without authorisation from the appropriate person within the organisation. You are providing outside parties with details of your organisation and only senior management will be able to judge whether this is appropriate.

4 Summary

In this chapter we have considered the general requirements of external agencies which might require a report or a return from your organisation. Normally the return required will be on a pre-printed form with clear instructions as to how to complete the form and the precise information that is required. Most figures will be in the form of either the standard performance indicators considered in the previous chapter or performance indicators that are clearly defined on the form itself.

CHAPTER 7

VAT – registration and administration

ASSESSMENT FOCUS

As well as being able to complete a VAT return you also need to understand how the VAT system works and the administration of VAT in order that you would be able to deal with the VAT office intelligently.

This chapter covers the following Knowledge and Understanding and Performance Criteria of the AAT Syllabus.

Relevant inputs and outputs are correctly identified and calculated (*Performance Criteria element 7.3*)

Guidance is sought from the VAT office when required, in a professional manner (*Performance Criteria element 7.3*)

Basic law and practice relating to all issues covered in the range statement and referred to in the performance criteria. Specific issues include: the classification of types of supply; registration requirements; the form of VAT invoices; tax points (*Knowledge and Understanding element 7.3*)

Sources of information on VAT: Customs and Excise Guide (*Knowledge and Understanding element 7.3*)

Administration of VAT: enforcement (*Knowledge and Understanding element 7.3*)

Special schemes: annual accounting; cash accounting; bad debt relief (*Knowledge and Understanding element 7.3*)

An understanding of the basis of the relationship between the organisation and the VAT office (*Knowledge and Understanding element 7.3*)

In order to cover these the following topics are included.

How the collection of VAT works

Registration for VAT

Types of supply – standard rated, zero rated and exempt

Partial exemption

Administration and enforcement of VAT

VAT records

Annual accounting scheme for VAT

Cash accounting scheme for VAT

1 Value added tax (VAT) – how it works

1.1 Introduction

Value added tax (VAT) is a European tax – it applies **throughout the European Community (EC).**

We are going to look at VAT within the **United Kingdom** only. The United Kingdom includes England and Wales, Scotland and Northern Ireland (but not the Channel Islands).

1.2 How does VAT work?

 **VAT is a tax paid by consumers** but it is collected by businesses on behalf of HM Customs and Excise.

♦ Businesses who make **taxable supplies** collect the tax from their customers. (The definition of **taxable supplies** is wider than just sales. It includes goods taken from the business for personal use.)

Definition   The VAT charged on sales or taxable supplies is known as **output VAT**.

♦ Those businesses **(taxable persons)** have to assess the amount of tax payable on goods and services provided **(output tax).** They pay it over on a regular basis to HM Customs and Excise.

♦ When a business makes purchases or pays expenses it will also be paying the VAT on those purchases/expenses.

Definition   VAT on purchases or expenses is known as **input VAT**.

♦ As the businesses themselves are not being taxed, they are allowed to reclaim tax on their own expenditure **(input VAT).**

 ♦ The input VAT is deducted from the output VAT and the net amount is paid each quarter to HM Customs & Excise, or recovered from them.

1.3 Example

A business makes sales of £10,000 plus £1,750 of VAT. Its expenditure totals £7,000 plus £1,225 of VAT. How much VAT is due to Customs and Excise?

1.4 Solution

	£
Output VAT	1,750
Less: Input VAT	1,225
VAT due	525

1.5 VAT place of supply

A **supply** must take place within the United Kingdom to be a **taxable supply** under United Kingdom VAT law.

Generally, if a business makes a **supply of goods from stocks held in the United Kingdom,** then the supply takes place in the United Kingdom. If the business must install the goods at the customer's premises, then the supply takes place at those premises.

When supplying services, the **place of supply is the place where the supplier belongs,** eg where a supplier has fixed business premises.

1.6   Time of supply

Most businesses account for input and output VAT according to the **dates that they issue and receive invoices.** The time of supply is known as the **tax point** and this is covered in more detail in the next chapter.

1.7   VAT Guide

Customs and Excise issue a booklet called the VAT Guide which is a guide to the main VAT rules and procedures. If you are dealing with accounting for VAT and VAT returns in practice then you should become familiar with the contents of the VAT Guide in order to be able to refer to it when necessary.

2   Registration for VAT

2.1   Compulsory registration

Anyone in business whose **taxable supplies exceed a certain annual limit** must register. This includes sole traders, partnerships and limited companies. Penalties for failing to register can be severe.

A **business must register** if:

♦ at the end of any month the value of taxable supplies in the past year has exceeded the annual limit of £54,000; or

♦ at any time there are reasonable grounds for believing that the value of taxable supplies to be made in the next 30 days will exceed the annual limit of £54,000; or

♦ their acquisitions from other EC member states are more than £54,000 in the calendar year.

2.2   Voluntary registration for VAT

A business may **volunteer to register for VAT.** HM Customs and Excise may refuse registration if the applicant is unable to show that supplies are being made in the course of business. The reason why someone might wish to voluntarily register for VAT will be considered later in the chapter.

2.3   More than one business

It is the **person not the business** which is required to register. So, if a person is carrying on several businesses, only a single registration is required and the turnovers of all businesses carried on by that person must be considered together when considering registration limits.

2.4   Example

Robert Parker is a sole trader with three businesses: a hairdressing business (taxable turnover £29,000 per annum), a printing business (taxable turnover £15,000 per annum) and he also deals in second-hand cars (taxable turnover £17,000 per annum). Does he have to register for VAT?

2.5   Solution

The VAT registration limit applies to the total taxable turnover of all the business interests of a taxable person. In this case each business venture is below the limit, but in total they exceed the limit. Robert Parker would have to register for VAT.

Let us now assume that the hairdressing business is a partnership with Peter Green. The partnership would be treated as a different taxable person from Robert Parker trading alone. Both taxable persons (Robert Parker and the partnership) would avoid registration

2.6   Deregistration for VAT

A taxable person may **deregister** if the value of his taxable supplies (net of VAT) is expected to be less than £52,000 in the following 12 months. If the taxable person changes – for example, when a sole trader incorporates – then the registration of the sole trader will be cancelled.

 If a person reaches the registration limit for VAT then they must register immediately. If not it is entirely possible that they will have to pay the VAT that should have been charged out of their own pockets.

3   Types of supply

3.1   Rates of VAT

There are three types of supply: **standard-rated** (with a reduced rate for domestic fuel and power), **zero-rated** and **exempt**. These are examples of zero-rated and exempt items.

Zero-rated	Exempt
♦ Water and most types of food	♦ Land (including rent on property)
♦ Books and newspapers	♦ Insurance
♦ Drugs and medicines	♦ Postal services
♦ Public transport	♦ Betting, gaming and lotteries
♦ Children's clothing and footwear	♦ Finance (eg making loans)
♦ Sewerage + water services	♦ Non profit-making education
♦ New house building	♦ Health services provided by doctors and dentists

All supplies that are not zero-rated or exempt are standard-rated at 17.5%. The exception is the supply of domestic fuel and power which is at a rate of 5%.

 The turnover limits for registration mentioned above include both zero-rated and standard-rated supplies. They do not include exempt supplies.

3.2   Zero rated and exempt supplies

 The distinction between zero rated supplies and exempt supplies is important. If a person makes zero rated supplies then input VAT can be reclaimed from Customs and Excise. However if a person makes exempt supplies he cannot register for VAT and therefore cannot reclaim any input tax from Customs and Excise.

3.3   Voluntary registration for VAT

The reason a person may voluntarily register for VAT is if they have zero rated supplies and wish to register in order to reclaim their input tax.

3.4   Partial exemption for VAT

A taxable person who makes both taxable supplies (standard and zero–rated) and exempt supplies is referred to as **'partially exempt'**. For this purpose, zero-rated supplies are treated as taxable. The problem which arises from partial exemption is that taxable supplies entitle the supplier to a credit for input tax, whereas exempt supplies do not. It is therefore necessary to identify an acceptable method of apportioning input tax between taxable and exempt supplies

 VAT can only be reclaimed if it is incurred in making taxable supplies.

3.5   Calculation of the input tax to be reclaimed

To calculate the **input tax attributable to an exempt supply the procedure is as follows:**

◆   Identify the person's **input tax**.

◆   Calculate the extent to which **that input tax relates to input supplies** which are wholly used or to be used by that person in making **taxable supplies** – this amount of input tax is reclaimable in full.

◆   Calculate the extent to which the input tax relates to input supplies which are wholly used or to be used by that person in making **exempt supplies** – this amount of input tax is disallowed in full.

◆   Calculate the **disallowable proportion of any remaining input tax**. The formula normally used for calculating the remaining input tax not reclaimable is:

$$\frac{\text{Value of exempt supplies}}{\text{Value of total supplies}} \times \text{Value of remaining input tax}$$

For convenience, the disallowable input tax will normally be added to the cost of sales but may be apportioned back over the items giving rise to the disallowable input tax.

3.6   Example

A trader pays £30,000 in input tax (purchase tax). This relates to:

	£
Wholly taxable supplies	18,000
Wholly exempt supplies	2,000
Other supplies	10,000
	30,000
Total taxable supplies	150,000
Total exempt supplies	50,000
	200,000

How much input tax can be reclaimed?

3.7   Solution

So what cannot be reclaimed?

$$\frac{\text{Value of exempt supplies}}{\text{Value of total supplies}} \times \text{remaining input tax} = \frac{£50,000}{£200,000} \times £10,000$$

$$= £2,500 \text{ not reclaimable}$$

So what can be reclaimed?

	£
Wholly taxable supplies	18,000
Remainder of other supplies (£10,000 – £2,500)	7,500
Reclaimable	25,500

3.8   Non-reclaimable input tax

There are some items of expense upon which VAT is charged but the VAT cannot be reclaimed from Customs and Excise. These include:

♦   business entertainment expenses

♦   purchase of a car for use within the business

♦   goods and services purchased but not used within the business ie used by the owner instead

---

Activity 1 *(The answer is in the final chapter of this book)*

In the most recent quarter a business has made standard rated supplies of £22,400 (net of VAT) and zero rated supplies of £5,500. The total of purchases and expenses on which VAT has been charged for the quarter are £16,300 (net of VAT).

How much VAT is due to or from Customs and Excise?

---

4   Administration of VAT

4.1   Introduction

The main source of law on VAT is the **VAT Act 1994**, the annual **Finance Acts** and other regulations issued by the government.

HM Customs and Excise is the government department that is responsible for administering VAT in the United Kingdom. VAT offices across the country are responsible for the local administration of VAT within a particular geographical area.

Officers from the **local VAT office** deal with registration, visit taxpayers to check returns and deal with routine enquiries. They are also responsible for enforcing the tax.

Taxpayers send their returns and payments to the **VAT Central Unit** at Southend-on-Sea that keeps central records.

4.2   Customs and Excise power

Customs and Excise have certain **powers** that help them administer the tax. They have the power to examine records, inspect premises, make assessments for underpaid tax and raise penalties for breaches of VAT law. Penalties may be made for (amongst other things) failing to register for VAT, failing to make returns or failing to make payments on time. They also decide whether or not supplies are liable to VAT.

The decisions of Customs and Excise are **not legally binding**.

There are inevitably **disputes between the taxpayer and Customs and Excise**. Customs and Excise have their own administrative procedures to deal with disputes. In certain cases the taxpayer may appeal to a VAT tribunal. The taxpayer may appeal against the decision of a VAT tribunal to the High Court (on a point of law only). Beyond that appeals may go to the Court of Appeal and then to the House of Lords. The ultimate legal authority on VAT is the European Court of Justice.

4.3   VAT records

The **form of records** must allow Customs and Excise to check VAT returns adequately. Generally, the business must keep records of:

♦   all taxable and exempt **supplies made** in the course of business

♦   all taxable **supplies received** in the course of business

♦   a summary of the total output tax and input tax for each tax period – the **VAT account** (see later chapter).

4.4   Details to be kept

The business must keep records to prove the figures shown on the VAT returns for **the previous six years.** These records might include the following:

♦   orders and delivery notes

♦   relevant business correspondence

♦   appointment and job books

♦   purchases and sales books

♦   cash books and other account books

♦   bank statements, paying-in slips and cheque stubs

♦   purchase invoices and copy sales invoices

♦   recordings of daily takings, including till rolls

♦   annual accounts

♦   import and export documents

♦   VAT accounts

♦   any credit notes issued or received

 Registered businesses may be visited by a VAT officer on occasion to ensure that their records are being correctly maintained.

A business can keep its records on **microfilm**. The business must tell Customs and Excise. It must be possible to inspect the records.

Any business that maintains its records on **computer** must tell Customs and Excise. The system must comply with VAT regulations.

Some businesses send or receive invoices by **electronic means**. Again they must tell Customs and Excise and check that they are complying with regulations.

 You must be able to list the records that must be kept for VAT purposes.

4.5   Special schemes

 Normally a VAT return is completed by a registered person every three months and any amounts of VAT due paid over to Customs and Excise with the return or a claim made for VAT to be reimbursed.

However there are some special schemes that are different – the two that you are required to be aware of for Unit 7 are the annual accounting scheme and the cash accounting scheme.

4.6   VAT: Annual accounting scheme

Under this scheme a VAT return is only made once a year rather than quarterly.

In order to qualify for this scheme the registered person must have annual taxable supplies of £600,000 or less. An estimate is made of the likely annual VAT due, this agreed figure is divided by 10, and nine equal monthly payments are made by direct debit, starting four months into the year.

The balance is then due with the annual VAT return within two months after the end of the VAT year.

The benefit of this scheme to a sole trader is that he does not have to spend valuable time every quarter completing a VAT return. However it does mean that his VAT records must be kept accurately as the VAT return is only completed once a year.

4.7   VAT: Cash accounting scheme

Normally VAT is due from the date invoices are sent out and can be reclaimed from the date a supplier's invoice is received (details in the next chapter). However under the cash accounting scheme a business accounts for VAT due on the basis of the time when the payment is actually received from customers or made to suppliers.

In order to qualify for this scheme the registered person must have expected annual taxable supplies of £600,000 or less and have a clean VAT record.

If registered under this scheme invoices will still be sent out to customers and received from suppliers but the key record that must be kept is a cash book summarising all payments made and received and their date with a separate column for VAT.

The benefit of this scheme is in terms of cash flow for a trader who must pay his suppliers promptly but has to wait a considerable time before being paid by his customers. It also means that there is automatic relief for VAT on bad debts because, if the customer does not pay, then the VAT is not due (bad debt relief in normal circumstances is considered in a later chapter).

5   Summary

This chapter has served as an introduction to the VAT system. You should now understand how VAT is collected by businesses but is a tax paid by the final consumer.

You must know when a person should register for VAT and deregister if relevant. You should also be clear as to the different types of supply and the difference to a trader between making zero rated supplies and exempt supplies.

We also considered how VAT is administered by local VAT officers and the documents and records that must be kept for six years in order to ensure that the correct amount of VAT has been paid.

Finally we considered two special schemes for VAT payment – the annual accounting scheme and the cash accounting scheme.

CHAPTER 8

VAT – invoices and tax points

ASSESSMENT FOCUS

You need to be aware of the details that must appear on a VAT invoice and the exceptions to the basic rule for invoicing. You also need to understand the rules regarding tax points as these will determine the time period in which output and input VAT is to be accounted for and therefore the figures that will eventually appear on the VAT return.

This chapter covers the following Knowledge and Understanding and Performance Criteria of the AAT Syllabus.

> Relevant inputs and outputs are correctly identified and calculated (*Performance Criteria element 7.3*)

> Basic law and practice relating to all issues covered in the range statement and referred to in the performance criteria. Specific issues include: the classification of types of supply; registration requirements; the form of VAT invoices; tax points (*Knowledge and Understanding element 7.3*)

In order to cover these the following topics are included.

> The details required on a VAT invoice

> VAT calculations and discounts

> Rounding VAT calculations

> Less detailed VAT invoices

> Modified invoices

> Pro-forma invoices

> Credit notes

> Tax points

1   VAT invoices

1.1   Introduction

All businesses that are registered for VAT must collect tax on taxable supplies. In order to do this the supplier must give or send to the purchaser a VAT invoice within 30 days of the supply.

1.2   Form of a VAT invoice

There is **no standard format for invoices**. The exact design is the choice of the business, but **it must show the following details** (unless the invoice is a **less detailed tax invoice** that you will see later):

♦ identifying number
♦ date of supply (or *tax point* – see below) and the date of issue of the invoice
♦ supplier's name and address and registration number
♦ name and address of customer, ie the person to whom the goods or services are supplied
♦ type of supply
  - sale
  - hire purchase, credit sale, conditional sale or similar transaction
  - loan
  - exchange
  - hire, lease or rental
  - process (making goods using the customer's own materials)
  - sale on commission (eg by an estate agent)
  - supply on sale or return
♦ description of the goods or services
♦ quantity of goods or extent of services.
♦ rate of tax and amount payable (in sterling) excluding VAT for each separate description
♦ total amount payable (excluding VAT) in sterling
♦ rate of any cash discount offered (these are also called settlement discounts)
♦ separate rate and amount of VAT charged for each rate of VAT
♦ total amount of VAT chargeable.

 A VAT invoice is not strictly required where the purchaser is not registered for VAT, however as the seller will not know whether a purchaser is registered, one will be sent.

1.3   *What a VAT invoice looks like*

Here is an example of a **tax invoice**.

MICRO TRAINING GROUP LTD
Unit 34
Castlewell Trading Estate
Manchester
M12 5RF

To: JF Jenkins & Co 65 Green Street Manchester M12 4ED	Sales invoice number: 35
	VAT registered number: 234 5566 87
	Tax point: 12 September 20X2

SALE

Quantity	Description and price	Amount ex VAT	VAT rate	VAT
6	Programmable calculators FR34 at £24.76	148.56	17.5%	
12	Programmable calculators GT60 at £36.80	441.60	17.5%	
		590.16		101.21
	Delivery	23.45	17.5%	4.02
Terms: Cash discount of 2% if paid within 10 days		613.61		105.23
VAT		105.23		
TOTAL		718.84		

1.4   VAT and discounts

 If a trade discount is given then this is deducted before the VAT is calculated. If a settlement discount is offered then the VAT is always calculated on the **lowest amount that the customer may pay**. You must assume that the customer will take the discount.

1.5   Example

In the above example a 2% cash discount is offered. Show how the VAT is calculated.

1.6   Solution

£613.61 × 98% × 17.5% = £105.23

 **Activity 1** *(The answer is in the final chapter of this book)*

An invoice is issued for standard rated goods with a list price of £380.00 (excluding VAT). A 10% trade discount is given and a 4% settlement or cash discount is offered.

How much VAT should be included on the invoice?

1.7   Rounding VAT

Usually, the amount of VAT calculated will not be a whole number of pounds and pence. You will therefore need a rounding adjustment. The rules governing this adjustment are quite tricky, and permit more than one method. For simplicity, the following approach is recommended.

♦   On an invoice containing several lines, where the VAT is shown separately for each line, calculate the amount of VAT for each line by rounding to the nearest 1p. For example, 87.7p would be rounded up to 88p. Then simply add up the VAT for each line to arrive at the total VAT.

♦   On an invoice containing just one (total) figure for VAT, calculate the amount of VAT by rounding *down* to the nearest 1p. For example £20.877 would be rounded down to £20.87.

 Activity 2 *(The answer is in the final chapter of this book)*

(a)   Given below is an extract from a VAT invoice:

Quantity	Description and price	Net of VAT	VAT rate	VAT
16	6 metre hosepipes @ £3.23	51.68	17.5%	
24	12 metre hosepipes @ £5.78	138.72	17.5%	

Calculate the VAT for each line of the invoice and the total VAT charged.

(b)   An invoice includes a net total for goods of £1,084.50. How much VAT should be charged for these goods?

1.8   Less detailed VAT invoices

Retailers do not have to issue a VAT invoice every time they make a sale. This would make trading impossible. If the total amount of the supply (including VAT) by the retailer does not exceed £100.00, a retailer may issue a **less detailed tax invoice**. However, if requested by a customer a full VAT invoice must be issued. The supplier only needs to show the following details on the invoice:

♦   supplier's name and address

♦   supplier's VAT registration number

♦   date of supply

♦   description sufficient to identify the goods or services

♦   amount payable (including VAT) for each rate (standard and zero)

♦   each rate of VAT

 The main differences here are that the customer's name and address can be omitted, and the total on the invoice includes the VAT without the VAT itself being shown separately.

Although this invoice shows less detail, it is still a valid **tax invoice**.

All retailers must keep a record of their **daily gross takings** so that VAT can be calculated on the total of cash takings, not individual invoices. This means that the retailer will need to keep a careful note of any money taken for own use.

1.9   Calculating the VAT

When a less detailed VAT invoice is issued or received it will be necessary to calculate the amount of the VAT that is included in the invoice total in order to record the sale or purchase in the accounting records.

The VAT element is calculated by multiplying the invoice total (for standard rated goods) by the fraction 17.5/117.5 or 7/47.

1.10   Example

If the VAT inclusive amount is £48.66 what is the VAT element?

1.11   Solution

$$\text{VAT} = 48.66 \times \frac{17.5}{117.5} = £7.24$$

or

$$\text{VAT} = 48.66 \times \frac{7}{47} = £7.24$$

 Remember that the VAT is rounded down to the next penny.

 ***Activity 3*** *(The answer is in the final chapter of this book)*

The total of a less detailed invoice for standard rated goods is £68.90. How much VAT is included in this amount?

1.12 Modified invoices

For a sale of any amount, if the buyer agrees, then a modified invoice can be issued. This shows the VAT inclusive amount for each item sold and then at the bottom of the invoice the following amounts must be shown:

♦ the overall VAT inclusive total

♦ the total amount of VAT included in the total

♦ the total value of the supplies net of VAT

♦ the total value of any zero rated and exempt supplies

1.13 Proforma invoices

When a business issues a sales invoice that includes VAT, the VAT becomes payable to Customs and Excise next time the business submits a return. This can cause cashflow problems if the customer has not yet paid the invoice, because the business then has to pay the VAT **before** collecting it from the customer.

To avoid this, a business may issue a **proforma invoice,** which essentially is a demand for payment. Once payment is received, the business will then issue a 'live' invoice to replace the proforma.

 Because a proforma invoice **does not rank as a VAT invoice** the supplier is **not** required to pay VAT to Customs and Excise until the 'live' invoice is issued. By the same token, the customer cannot reclaim the VAT on a proforma invoice, but must instead wait until the valid tax invoice is received.

Pro-forma invoices should be clearly marked "THIS IS NOT A VAT INVOICE".

1.14 Credit notes and VAT

A **credit note** involving a taxable supply must show:

♦ the identifying number and date of issue

♦ the supplier's name, address and registration number

♦ the customer's name and address

♦ the reason for the credit (eg goods returned)

♦ a description of the goods or services for which the credit is being allowed

♦ the quantity and amount credited for each description

♦ the total amount credited, excluding VAT

♦ the rate and amount of VAT credited.

The **number and date of the original tax** invoice should also appear on the credit note.

If the supplier issues the credit note without making a VAT adjustment the credit note must say: **'This is not a credit note for VAT'.**

A supplier is **not allowed to issue a credit note to recover VAT on bad debts.** See the section in Chapter 9 on bad debts for the detailed procedures.

2 Tax points

2.1 Introduction

Definition The **tax point** is the date on which the liability for output tax arises – it is the date on which it is recorded as taking place for the purposes of the tax return.

Most taxable persons make a VAT return each quarter. The return must include all supplies whose tax points fall within that quarter.

2.2 The basic tax point

 The 'basic tax point' is the date of delivery of goods or the date the customer takes the goods away or the date of completion/performance of services.

2.3 Actual tax point

Where an invoice is issued or payment received before the basic tax point, **this earlier date becomes the 'actual tax point'.**

If a supplier issues an invoice within 14 days after the basic tax point, the invoice date becomes the actual tax point and is used as the tax point for the tax return, unless payment has been received earlier, in which case the payment date is the actual tax point.

Provided that written approval is received from the local VAT office the 14 day rule can be varied, for example to accommodate a supplier who issues all of his invoices each month on the last day of the month.

2.4 Deposits received in advance

Any **deposits received in advance** create a basic tax point. The business must account for the VAT element. The VAT included in the deposit must be calculated and entered in the accounting records.

2.5 Example

A £50.00 deposit is received in advance of the goods being delivered. What is the VAT on this amount?

2.6 Solution

The amount of VAT included in the deposit = £50.00 $\times \dfrac{7}{47}$ = £7.44.

 ***Activity 4*** *(The answer is in the final chapter of this book)*

In each of the following cases state the date of the tax point and whether it is a basic tax point or actual tax point:

(i) Goods delivered to a customer on 10 July, invoice sent out on 15 July and payment received on 30 July.

(ii) Invoice sent out to a customer on 12 August, goods delivered to the customer on 16 August, payment received 20 September.

(iii) Payment received from customer on 4 September, goods sent to customer on 5 September together with the invoice.

(iv)   Goods delivered to a customer on 13 September, invoice sent out on 30 September and payment received on 31 October.

3   *Summary*

This chapter has covered two important areas for VAT – invoicing and tax points. VAT invoices must include certain details and in normal circumstances must be given or sent to a VAT registered purchaser. In practice this means that all purchasers will be provided with a VAT invoice whether they are registered or not. However, retailers are allowed to issue less detailed or modified invoices if the customer is happy with this, showing only the total amount due without any breakdown of the VAT included. Any credit notes sent out by a business must include the same details as the invoices.

The tax point for a supply of goods is important as this determines the date on which the VAT becomes accountable therefore determining which VAT return the VAT for that supply of goods appears on. You must know the rules for the basic tax point and for actual tax points.

CHAPTER 9

VAT returns

ASSESSMENT FOCUS

In many assessments you will be required to fill out a VAT return ready for authorisation and despatch. There are a number of boxes to complete on the VAT return and you need to know where to find the appropriate figures.

This chapter covers the following Knowledge and Understanding and Performance Criteria of the AAT Syllabus.

VAT returns are correctly completed using data from the appropriate recording systems and are submitted within the statutory time limits (*Performance Criteria element 7.3*)

Submissions are made in accordance with current legislation (*Performance Criteria element 7.3*)

Guidance is sought from the VAT office when required, in a professional manner (*Performance Criteria element 7.3*)

Special schemes: annual accounting; cash accounting; bad debt relief (*Knowledge and Understanding element 7.3*)

An understanding of the basis of the relationship between the organisation and the VAT office (*Knowledge and Understanding element 7.3*)

In order to cover these the following topics are included.

When a VAT return should be completed
What a VAT return looks like
Treatment of exports and imports
The VAT account
Other information required for completing the VAT return
Step by step approach to completing the VAT return
Adjustment for errors on previous VAT returns
Bad debt relief
Customs and Excise penalties

1　The VAT return

1.1　Introduction

The tax period for VAT is **three months,** or one month for taxpayers who choose to make monthly returns (normally taxpayers who receive regular refunds).

The taxpayer must complete a **VAT return (a VAT 100 form) at the end of each quarter.** The return summarises all the transactions for the period.

1.2　Timing of the VAT return

 The taxpayer must make the return within **one month of the end of the tax period.** The taxable person must send the amount due at the same time (ie. output tax collected less input tax deducted). Payment may be by cheque (made payable to HM Customs and Excise and crossed) or by credit transfer.

If VAT is due from Customs and Excise the VAT return must still be completed and submitted within one month of the end of the quarter in order to be able to reclaim the amount due.

1.3   *What a VAT return looks like*

Given below is an example of a VAT return:

Value Added Tax Return
For the period

	For Official Use

Registration number	Period

You could be liable to a financial penalty
if your completed return and all the VAT
payable are not received by the due date.

Due date:

For Official Use	

Your VAT Office telephone number is 0123-4567

Before you fill in this form please read the notes on the back and the VAT Leaflet '*Filling in your VAT return*'. Fill in all boxes clearly in ink and write 'none' where necessary. Don't put a dash or leave any box blank If there are no pence write '00' in the pence column. Do not enter more than one amount in any box.

For official use				
	VAT due in this period on sales and other outputs	1		
	VAT due in this period on acquisitions from other EC Member states	2		
	Total VAT due (the sum of boxes 1 and 2)	3		
	VAT reclaimed in this period on purchases and other inputs (including acquisitions from the EC)	4		
	Net VAT to be paid to Customs or reclaimed by you (Difference between boxes 3 and 4)	5		
	Total value of sales and all other outputs excluding any VAT. Include your box 8 figure.	6		00
	Total value of purchases and all other inputs excluding any VAT. Include your box 9 figure.	7		00
	Total value of all supplies of goods and related services excluding any VAT to other EC Member States.	8		00
	Total value of all supplies of goods and related services excluding any VAT, from other EC Member States.	9		00

Retail schemes. If you have used any of the schemes in the period covered by this return, enter the relevant letter(s) in this box.

If you are enclosing a payment please tick this box	DECLARATION You or someone on your behalf must sign below.
	I .... declare that the information given
	(Full name of signatory in BLOCK LETTERS)
	above is true and complete.
	Signature .... Date 20
	A false declaration can result in prosecution.

As you will see there are nine boxes to complete with the relevant figures. Boxes 2, 8 and 9 are to do with supplies of goods and services to other European Community (EC) Member States and acquisitions from EC Member States. Therefore we will now consider how VAT is affected by exports and imports.

1.4   VAT: Exports and imports to or from non-EC members

Generally, goods **exported** from the United Kingdom are normally **zero rated** (ie there is no tax charged on them, even if there normally would be) provided there is documentary evidence of the export.

Goods that are **imported** from outside the EC have to have customs duty paid on them when they enter the country. Goods that would be taxed at the standard rate of VAT if supplied in the United Kingdom are also subject to VAT. The tax is collected in the same way as customs duties. The amount payable is based on their value including duty. This applies to all goods whether or not they are for business use. The aim of the charge is to treat foreign goods in the same way as home-produced goods.

If the imported goods are for business use and the business uses them to make taxable supplies, it can reclaim the VAT paid in the usual way as input tax on the VAT return.

1.5   The EC system

Movements of goods between EC Member States are no longer known as imports and exports but as acquisitions. Any VAT is collected from the **buyer** of the goods.

A VAT registered buyer of goods (acquisitions) has to pay the VAT due on the goods, at the rate that applies in the buyer's country, and the buyer can then treat the VAT as input tax on the VAT return.

This means that on the VAT return a UK buyer of goods, acquisitions, from another EC state must pay the VAT due at the UK rate to Customs and Excise. This is done by including the VAT due on the goods as output tax in Box 2 of the VAT return. The VAT due on the goods is then also treated as input tax in Box 4 which includes the VAT on acquisitions from EC Member States.

2   Completing the VAT return

2.1   The VAT account

The main source of information for the VAT return is the VAT account which must be maintained to show the amount that is due to or from Customs and Excise at the end of each quarter.

2.2   How the VAT account should look

Given below is a pro-forma of a VAT account as suggested by the VAT Guide.

1 April 20X5 to 30 June 20X5

VAT deductible - input tax		VAT payable - output tax	
VAT on purchases		VAT on sales	
April	X	April	X
May	X	May	X
June	X	June	X
VAT on imports	X		
VAT on acquisition from EC	X	VAT on acquisition from EC	X
Adjustments of previous errors (if £2,000 or less)			
Net underclaim	X	Net overclaim	X
Bad debt relief	X		
Less: Credit notes received	(X)	Less: Credit notes issued	(X)
Total tax deductible	X	Total tax payable	X
		Less: total tax deductible	(X)
		Payable to Customs and Excise	X

You will note that the VAT shown is not strictly a double entry account as the VAT on credit notes received is deducted from input tax and the VAT on credit notes issued is deducted from output tax instead of being credited and debited respectively.

2.3   Information required for the VAT return

Boxes 1 to 4 of the VAT return can be fairly easily completed from the information in the VAT account. However, Boxes 6 and 7 require figures for total sales and purchases excluding VAT. This information will need to be extracted from the totals of the accounting records such as sales day book and purchases day book totals.

Boxes 8 and 9 require figures, excluding VAT, for the value of supplies to other EC Member States and acquisitions from other EC Member States. Therefore the accounting records should be designed in such a way that these figures can also be easily identified.

Activity 1 *(The answer is in the final chapter of this book)*

Panther

You are preparing the VAT return for Panther Alarms Ltd and you must first identify the sources of information for the VAT account.

Suggest the best sources of information for the following figures:

(a)   Sales

(b)   Credit notes issued

(c)   Purchases

(d)   Credit notes received

(e)   Capital goods sold

(f)   Capital goods purchased

(g)   Goods taken from business for own use

(h)   Bad debt relief

2.4   Example

Given below is a VAT account for Thompson Brothers for the second VAT quarter of 20X5.

Thompson Brothers Ltd

1 April 20X5 to 30 June 20X5

VAT deductible - input tax		VAT payable - output tax	
VAT on purchases	£	VAT on sales	£
April	525.00	April	875.00
May	350.00	May	1,750.00
June	350.00	June	700.00
	1,225.00		3,325.00
EC acquisitions	210.00	EC acquisitions	210.00
Other adjustments			
Less: Credit notes received	(17.50)	Less: Credit notes issued	(105.00)
Total tax deductible	1,417.50	Total tax payable	3,430.00
		Less: Total tax deductible	(1,417.50)
		Payable to Customs and Excise	2,012.50

You are also given the summarised totals from the day books for the three month period:

Sales Day Book

	Net £	VAT £	Total £
Standard rated	19,000.00	3,325.00	22,325.00
Zero rated	800.00	-	800.00
EC Member States	1,500.00	-	1,500.00

Sales Returns Day Book

	Net £	VAT £	Total £
Standard rated	600.00	105.00	705.00
Zero rated	40.00	-	40.00
EC Member States	-	-	-

Purchases Day Book

	Net £	VAT £	Total £
Standard rated	7,000.00	1,225.00	8,225.00
Zero rated	2,000.00	-	2,000.00
EC Member States	1,200.00	210.00	1,410.00

Purchases Returns Day Book

	Net £	VAT £	Total £
Standard rated	100.00	17.50	117.50
Zero rated	-	-	-
EC Member States	-	-	-

We also need the address and VAT registration number of the business:

Thompson Brothers Ltd
Arnold House
Parkway
Keele
KE4 8VS

VAT registration number 165 4385 32.

We are now in a position to complete the VAT return.

2.5   Solution

Step 1

Fill in the VAT registration number, VAT period, name and address of the business and the due date of the return which is one month after the end of the quarter.

Step 2

Fill in Box 1 with the VAT on sales less the VAT on credit notes issued - this can be taken either from the VAT account or from the day book summaries: £3,325 - £105 = £3,220.00.

Note that the instructions at the top of VAT return require '00' to be shown if there are no pence in the total.

Step 3

Fill in Box 2 with the VAT payable on acquisitions from other EC Member States - this figure of £210.00 can be taken either from the VAT account or from the Purchases Day Book.

Note that this figure will be included here on the VAT return as output tax payable to Customs and Excise and also in Box 4 as input tax reclaimable.

Step 4

Complete Box 3 with the total of Boxes 1 and 2.

Step 5

Fill in Box 4 with the total of VAT on all purchases (including acquisitions from EC Member States) less the total VAT on any credit notes received. These figures can either be taken from the VAT account or from the day book totals: £1,225.00 + £210.00 - £17.50 = £1,417.50.

Step 6

Complete Box 5 by deducting the figure in Box 4 from the total in Box 3. This is the amount due to Customs and Excise and should equal the balance on the VAT account.

If the Box 4 figure is larger than the Box 3 total then there is more input tax reclaimable than output tax to pay - this means that this is the amount being reclaimed from Customs and Excise.

Step 7

Fill in Box 6 with the VAT exclusive figure of all sales less credit notes issued - this information will come from the day books - this figure includes sales to EC Member States: £19,000 + £800.00 + £1,500.00 - £600.00 - £40.00 = £20,660.

Note that this figure includes zero rated supplies and any exempt supplies that are made.

Step 8

Fill in Box 7 with the VAT exclusive total of all purchases less credit notes received - again this will be taken from the day books: £7,000 + £2,000 + £1,200.00 - £100.00 = £10,100.00.

Step 9

Fill in Box 8 with the VAT exclusive total of all supplies made to EC Member States (less any credit notes) - this figure is taken from the Sales Day Book: £1,500.00.

Step 10

Fill in Box 9 with the VAT exclusive total of all acquisitions from other EC Member States (less any credit notes) - this figure is taken from the Purchases Day Book: £1,200.00.

Note that no pence are required for the final four boxes. Also note the instruction that if there is no entry for any box then 'none' should be written in the box.

Step 11

Write in the name of the person within the organisation (senior management or owner) who will be authorising the VAT return with their signature.

Step 12

If VAT is due to Customs and Excise a cheque must be sent with the VAT return and the box at the bottom of the return must be ticked.

Value Added Tax Return
For the period

1/4/X5 to 30/6/X5

For Official Use

Registration number	Period
165 4385 32	20X5

```
Thompson Brothers Ltd
Arnold House
Parkway
Keele
KE4 8VS
```

You could be liable to a financial penalty if your completed return and all the VAT payable are not received by the due date.

Due date: 31 July 20X5

For Official Use	

Your VAT Office telephone number is 0123-4567

Before you fill in this form please read the notes on the back and the VAT Leaflet *'Filling in your VAT return'*. Fill in all boxes clearly in ink and write 'none' where necessary. Don't put a dash or leave any box blank If there are no pence write '00' in the pence column. Do not enter more than one amount in any box.

For official use				
	VAT due in this period on sales and other outputs	1	3,220	00
	VAT due in this period on acquisitions from other EC Member states	2	210	00
	Total VAT due (the sum of boxes 1 and 2)	3	3.430	00
	VAT reclaimed in this period on purchases and other inputs (including acquisitions from the EC)	4	1,417	50
	Net VAT to be paid to Customs or reclaimed by you (Difference between boxes 3 and 4)	5	2,012	50
	Total value of sales and all other outputs excluding any VAT. Include your box 8 figure.	6	20,660	00
	Total value of purchases and all other inputs excluding any VAT. Include your box 9 figure.	7	10,100	00
	Total value of all supplies of goods and related services excluding any VAT to other EC Member States.	8	1,500	00
	Total value of all supplies of goods and related services excluding any VAT, from other EC Member States.	9	1,200	00
	Retail schemes. If you have used any of the schemes in the period covered by this return, enter the relevant letter(s) in this box.			

If you are enclosing a payment please tick this box	DECLARATION You or someone on your behalf must sign below.
✓	I ....A. THOMPSON.. declare that the information given (Full name of signatory in BLOCK LETTERS) above is true and complete. Signature .... Date 20 **A false declaration can result in prosecution.**

If the business makes sales or purchases for cash then the relevant net and VAT figures from the cash receipts and payments books should also be included on the VAT return.

Activity 2 *(The answer is in the final chapter of this book)*

Given below is a summary of the day books of a business for the three months ended 31 March 20X1. The business is called Long Supplies Ltd and trades from Vale House, Lilly Road, Trent, TR5 2KL. The VAT registration number of the business is 285 3745 12.

Sales Day Book

	Net £	VAT £	Total £
Standard rated	15,485.60	2,709.98	18,195.58
Zero rated	1,497.56	-	1,497.56

Sales Returns Day Book

	Net £	VAT £	Total £
Standard rated	1,625.77	284.50	1,910.27
Zero rated	106.59	-	106.59

Purchases Day Book

	Net £	VAT £	Total £
Standard rated	8,127.45	1,422.30	9,549.75
Zero rated	980.57	-	980.57
EC Member States	669.04	117.08	786.12

Purchases Returns Day Book

	Net £	VAT £	Total £
Standard rated	935.47	163.70	1,099.17
Zero rated	80.40	-	80.40
EC Member States	-	-	-

Required

(a)   Write up the VAT account to reflect these figures.

(b)   Complete the VAT return given.

Value Added Tax Return
For the period

For Official Use

Registration number   Period

You could be liable to a financial penalty if your completed return and all the VAT payable are not received by the due date.

Due date:

For Official Use	

Your VAT Office telephone number is 0123–4567

Before you fill in this form please read the notes on the back and the VAT Leaflet *'Filling in your VAT return'*. Fill in all boxes clearly in ink and write 'none' where necessary. Don't put a dash or leave any box blank If there are no pence write '00' in the pence column. Do not enter more than one amount in any box.

For official use			
	VAT due in this period on sales and other outputs	**1**	
	VAT due in this period on acquisitions from other EC Member states	**2**	
	Total VAT due (the sum of boxes 1 and 2)	**3**	
	VAT reclaimed in this period on purchases and other inputs (including acquisitions from the EC)	**4**	
	Net VAT to be paid to Customs or reclaimed by you (Difference between boxes 3 and 4)	**5**	
	Total value of sales and all other outputs excluding any VAT. Include your box 8 figure.	**6**	00
	Total value of purchases and all other inputs excluding any VAT. Include your box 9 figure.	**7**	00
	Total value of all supplies of goods and related services excluding any VAT to other EC Member States.	**8**	00
	Total value of all supplies of goods and related services excluding any VAT, from other EC Member States.	**9**	00

Retail schemes. If you have used any of the schemes in the period covered by this return, enter the relevant letter(s) in this box.

If you are enclosing a payment please tick this box	DECLARATION You or someone on your behalf must sign below.
	I .... declare that the information given
	(Full name of signatory in BLOCK LETTERS)
	above is true and complete.
	Signature .... Date 20
	A false declaration can result in prosecution.

2.6   VAT: Adjustment of previous errors

You will notice in the pro-forma VAT account that there are entries for net underclaims and net overclaims. Net errors made in previous VAT returns of £2,000 or less can be adjusted for on the VAT return through the VAT account.

Definition   Net error means the difference between any earlier errors in output tax and any earlier errors in input tax.

 The one single figure for net errors will then be entered as additional input tax if there has been an earlier net underclaim of VAT and as additional output tax if the net error was a net overclaim in a previous return.

2.7   Errors of more than £2,000

If the net error from a previous return totals more than £2,000 then the VAT office should be informed immediately either by a letter or on Form VAT 652. This is known as voluntary disclosure. The information provided to the VAT office should be:

◆   the amount of the error

◆   the VAT period in which it occurred

◆   whether the error was involving input or output tax

◆   whether the error is in favour of the business or Customs and Excise.

2.8   VAT: Bad debt relief

You will notice that there is an entry in the pro-forma VAT account for bad debt relief as additional input tax.

When a supplier invoices a customer for an amount including VAT, the supplier must pay the VAT to Customs and Excise. If the customer then fails to pay the debt, the supplier's position is that he has paid output VAT which he has never collected. This is obviously unfair, and the system allows him to recover such amounts.

We saw in Chapter 8 that **suppliers cannot issue credit notes to recover VAT on bad debts.**

Instead, the business must make an **adjustment through the VAT return.**

 The business can reclaim VAT already paid over if:

◆   output tax was paid on the original supply;

◆   six months have elapsed between the date of supply and the date of the VAT return; and

◆   the debt has been written off as a bad debt in the accounting records.

If the business receives a **repayment of the debt later,** it must make an adjustment to the VAT relief claimed.

3   VAT penalties

3.1   Late notification

 If a trader **trades in excess of the registration limits** without informing HM Customs & Excise, a penalty is levied for failing to register by the proper date.

This penalty is a **proportion of the net tax due** from the date registration should have taken place. The proportion percentage varies as follows:

Period of failure to register	Percentage of tax
9 months or less	5%
Over 9 months, but not over 18 months	10%
Over 18 months	15%

A **minimum penalty** of £50 exists. If the trader can show a reasonable excuse for not registering, the penalty may be mitigated.

3.2   Default surcharge

A **default** occurs when a trader submits his VAT return late or submits the return on time but pays the VAT late. On default, HM Customs & Excise serve a **default liability notice** on the taxpayer which identifies a surcharge period which runs from the date of the notice until the anniversary of the end of the period for which the taxpayer is in default.

If a **second default** occurs in the surcharge period it is further extended until the anniversary of the end of the period to which the new default relates.

If **VAT is paid late in a surcharge period**, a surcharge is payable as follows:

Default involving late payment of VAT in the surcharge period	Surcharge, % of outstanding VAT
1st	2%
2nd	5%
3rd	10%
4th and above	15%

(The minimum charge is £30.)

3.3   Misdeclaration penalties

Making returns which **understate the trader's VAT liability** incurs a penalty of 15 per cent of the lost tax. Errors of up to £2,000 can be rectified on the usual quarter-end VAT 100 return.

3.4   Default interest

Interest is charged on VAT due on an assessment from HM Customs & Excise. Interest runs from the date the VAT should have been paid (up to a maximum of three years).

4   Summary

In this final chapter the actual completion of the VAT return was considered. A business should keep a VAT account which summarises all of the VAT from the accounting records and this can be used to complete the first five boxes on the VAT return. The figure for VAT due to or from Customs and Excise on the VAT return should equal the balance on the VAT account.

In order to complete the remaining boxes on the VAT return information will be required from the accounting records of the business, normally in the form of the day books.

CHAPTER 10

Solutions to chapter activities

Chapter 1

1   Employment information

   (i)   Numbers employed.

   (ii)   Vacancies.

   (iii)   Hours worked, etc.

2   Agency return

   (a)   Return to trade associations, returns to government agencies, etc (eg VAT return).

   (b)   Compliance requirement, statistical trends and seasonal variations.

3   Employment Gazette

   (a)   Employment and unemployment details – where to locate a new factory.

   (b)   Earnings – how does the company compare with national averages?

Chapter 2

1 Finding the right word

In the following sentences, the words printed in italics in the question have been replaced by more suitable words (usually to avoid malapropisms):

(a) One statesman thought the treaty *derogatory* to his country's honour.

(b) The Frenchman regards the *observance* of the Sabbath from a different standpoint.

(c) The town officials did their best to make the buses popular and *profitable*.

(d) Among the typists she raised such *dissension* that no pair of them remained on speaking terms.

(e) Your best plan is to treat him as *contemptuously* as you can.

(f) The body was so mangled that it could hardly be recognised as *human*.

(g) It seemed that the patient ought to *die*.

(h) The girl was *nostalgic*.

(i) By these remarks do you mean to *imply* that I know something about your savings?

(j) I have photographed the children of that school now for 30 years without a *break*.

(k) The island is famous for its *luxuriant* vegetation.

(l) The murderer was seen in the very *act* of firing his gun.

(m) After the *discovery* of chloroform surgical operations had a higher rate of success.

2 Not at all obvious

Part (a)

To: Mrs Jenkins

SURVEY REPORT COMPARING THE ABILITY OF TWO TYPES OF DISPLAY STAND TO GENERATE SALES OF CARDS

Introduction

The object of this report is to compare two types of display stand by analysing their ability to generate sales of cards in newsagents.

The first type of card stand is the traditional one. This is five feet wide, made from formica with sloping perspex divisions.

The second type is the revolving metal card stand. This is two feet in diameter.

For the purpose of this report we will call them Traditional and Revolving.

Procedure

The survey was carried out in three cities, Bristol, Aberdeen and Manchester. The results shown in this report are those from Bristol.

Ten newsagents from Bristol were studied over a period of six working days, the 15th to 20th March. Half of these newsagents have the traditional stand to display cards and the other half have the revolving card stand. Details of the names and addresses of all ten shops are in the Appendix. For easier comparison the shops have been allocated letters from A to E.

Findings

The following table shows the number of cards sold over the six days in Bristol:

Shop	Traditional card sales	Shop	Revolving card sales
A		B	
C		E	435
D		F	475
G	286	H	575
I	275	J	525

The findings were similar in the other two cities chosen for the survey.

Conclusion

The higher numbers of cards sold are all in shops which use the revolving card stands.

Part (b)

MEMORANDUM

To:	Jo Bloggs	**Date:**	
From:	A Clerk		

Report on comparison of display stands and their ability to generate sales

Having read your survey report there are a number of questions that I would like you to answer:

1   How and why were the three cities chosen?

2   How and why were the ten newsagents in Bristol chosen?

3   Only six results are shown out of the ten shops studied. Where are the results from the others?

4   Are the figures for Aberdeen and Manchester available?

5   Have you considered exchanging Traditional for Revolving stands to determine whether the higher level of sales is a function of the type of stand or the size and location of the shop?

Chapter 3

1   Bunny and Hutch

Employees and wages of Bunny and Hutch Ltd 20X4

	Number of employees		Average weekly wage	Total annual wage bill
	1 Jan	31 Dec	£	£
Men	2,088	2,124	121.32	12,774,996
Women	1,871	1,860	87.93	8,201,671
Total	3,959	3,984	105.91	20,976,667

Workings

Number of women employed at 31 December	=	3,984 – 2,124 = 1,860
Number of men employed at 1 January	=	2,124 – 221 + 185 = 2,088
Number of women employed at 1 January	=	1,860 – 97 + 108 = 1,871
Total number employed at 1 January	=	2,088 + 1,871 = 3,959
Average number of men in year	=	(2,088 + 2,124) ÷ 2 = 2,106
Average number of women in year	=	(1,871 + 1,860) ÷ 2 = 1,865.5
Total annual wage bill for men	=	2,106 × 121.32 × 50 = £12,774,996
Total annual wage bill for women	=	1,865.5 × 87.93 × 50 = £8,201,671
Total annual wage bill	=	12,774,996 + 8,201,671 = £20,976,667

These estimates of the annual wage bill can be obtained in other ways. We could alternatively have used the 1 January figures of number employed or 31 December figures.

To calculate the total average weekly wage we could simply add £121.32 to £87.93 and divide by two. However, this assumes an equal number of men and women employees. Alternatively, since we now have an estimate of the total wage bill, the average weekly wage can be calculated as:

$$\frac{£20,976,667}{3,971.5 \times 50} = £105.64$$

2   Motor policies

The region with the highest number of policies held was London and this region also had the largest number of claims made in 20X3. The region with the smallest number of policies held was Northern Ireland, although this region had quite a high number of claims, being fifth highest of the eight regions. The smallest number of claims made was in Scotland which had the second smallest number of policy-holders.

Since the number of policies held in the different regions varies, more information can be gained by calculating the percentage number of claims per policies held for the eight regions.

Region	Claims per policies held (%)
North	8.2
Midlands	7.6
South	6.1
East Anglia	2.5
London	4.3
Wales	1.8
Scotland	1.6
Northern Ireland	10.5

From this table we can see that, although London had the highest actual number of claims, it is only the fourth highest in terms of claims as a proportion of policies held. In fact, Northern Ireland has the highest number of claims per policies held, whereas Scotland has the lowest number of claims per policies held.

3   WMSC

Part (a)

Key	Letter	November % 20X6	% 20X5
Wages and salaries	A	30	25
Building occupation costs	B	20	25
Agents' commission	E	25	20
General admin expenses	D	10	15
Depreciation	C	15	15
		100	100

Part (b)

To: Admin Manager

From: Assistant accountant

Subject: November pie charts   Date: 6 December 20X6

(1)   It is important to stress that in this comparison it is the relative size of the expenses that we are comparing.

(2)   Wages and salaries with building occupation costs amount to 50% of the total expenditure for each year but the proportion has changed by wages increasing and building costs reducing.

(3)   The proportion of agents commission has increased in November 20X6 and general admin expenses has reduced.

(4)   Depreciation is the same proportion in both years.

(5)   The agents' commission may have increased because the volume of sales increased (a variable expense). The general administration expenses may have

reduced due to more work being tackled in-house rather than by a bureau, eg computing. (This is backed-up by an increase in wages and salaries in 20X6.)

(Other reasons could be stated in answer to 5 above.)

4   Engineering assets

(a)

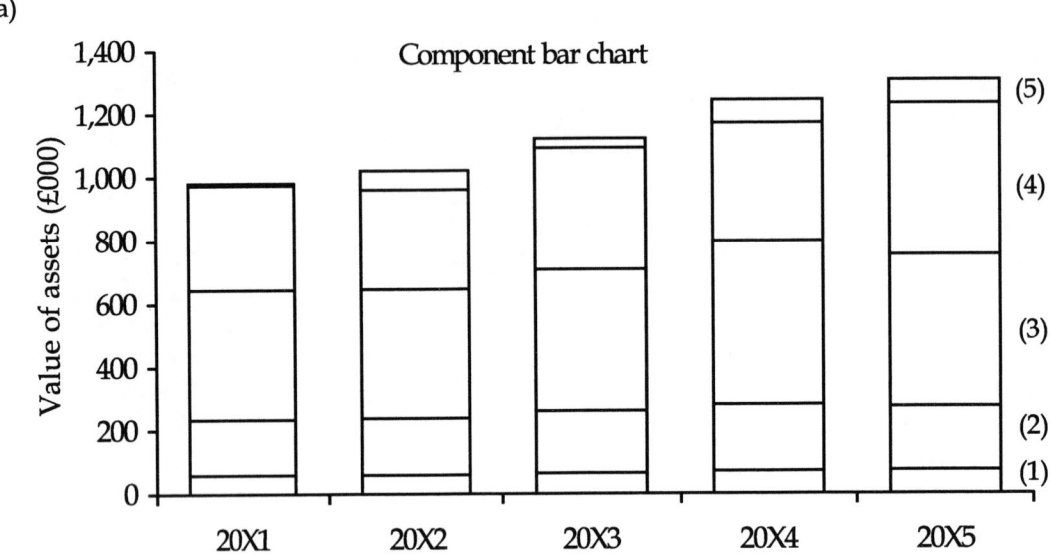

Key

(1)   Property

(2)   Plant and machinery

(3)   Stock and work in progress

(4)   Debtors

(5)   Cash

To construct a percentage component bar chart, we need to calculate the value of each of the assets as a percentage of the total, as follows.

Asset	20X1 £000	%	20X2 £000	%	20X3 £000	%	20X4 £000	%	20X5 £000	%
Property	59	6.0	59	5.8	65	5.8	70	5.6	74	5.7
Plant and machinery	176	17.9	179	17.5	195	17.4	210	16.9	200	15.3
Stock and WIP	409	41.7	409	40.1	448	40.0	516	41.5	479	36.7
Debtors	330	33.6	313	30.7	384	34.2	374	30.1	479	36.6
Cash	7	0.8	60	5.9	29	2.6	74	5.9	74	5.7
	981		1,020		1,121		1,244		1,306	

Percentage component bar chart

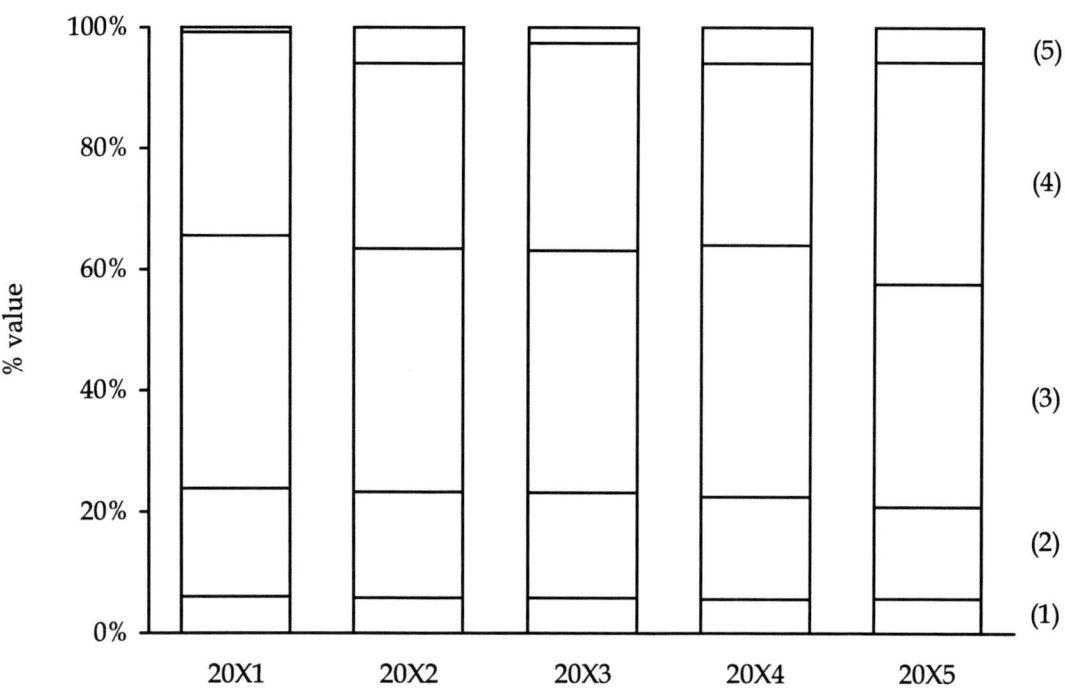

(b)   The total value of assets in 20X1 is £981,000

The total value of assets in 20X5 is £1,306,000.

This represents an increase in the five-year period of £325,000. The percentage increase in the total value of assets

$$= \frac{325,000}{981,000} \times 100 = 33.1\%$$

(c)   **Memorandum**

To: Mr Joseph

From: A Clerk   **Date**:

Subject: Movements in the assets over the five-year period

From the bar chart it is evident that there has been a yearly increase in total assets over the five-year period.

There have been some very small increases in the property component (1) and this component has remained a similar percentage of the total assets throughout the period.

The plant and machinery component (2) shows an increase over the first four years and a decrease in the fifth year. The stock and work in progress component (3) is larger than the plant and machinery component, but behaves in a similar way. Both have decreased as a percentage of total assets over the five years.

Both the debtor component (4) and the cash component (5) have increased since 20X1 but there is some variation in the figures.

Both debtors and cash increased as a percentage of total assets, but this was not a steady increase. The debtors percentage fell from 20X1 to 20X2 and then again from 20X3 to 20X4 whilst the cash percentage fell from 20X2 to 20X3.

5   Energy consumption

We first need to calculate the total energy consumption for each year (in millions of tonnes of coal equivalent).

20X1 Total consumption = 139.3 + 151.2 + 28.8 = 319.3

20X9 Total consumption = 129.6 + 139.0 + 71.3 = 339.9

(a)   **Component bar chart**

UK Inland energy consumption 20X1 and 20X9

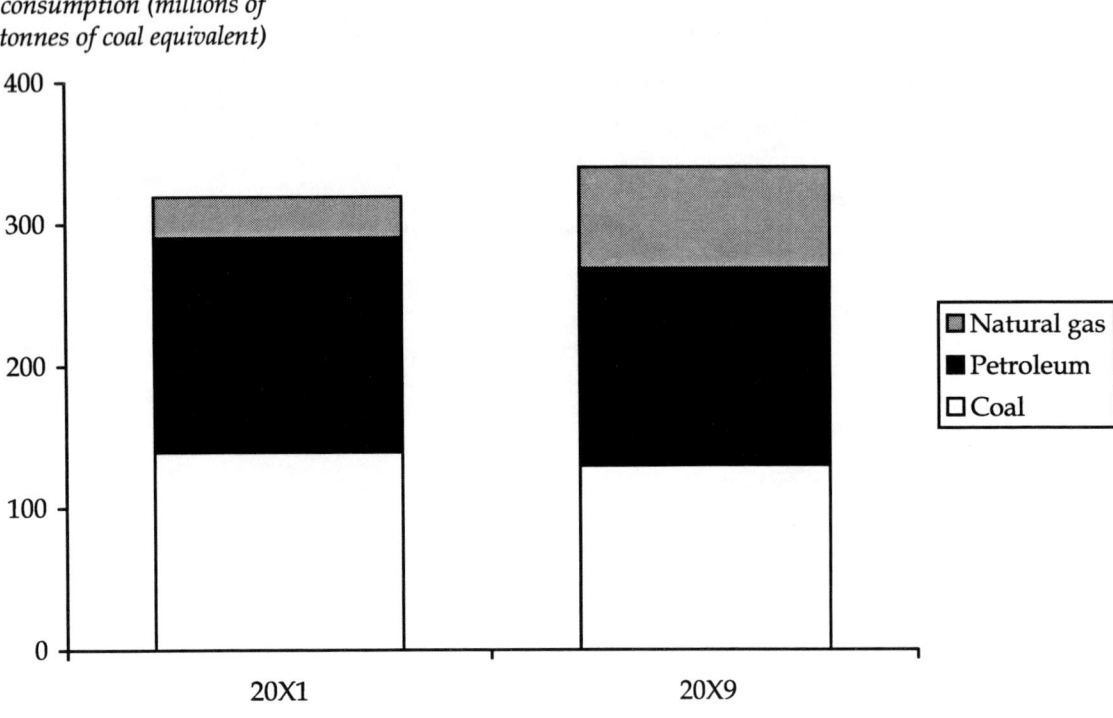

(b)   **Compound bar chart**

UK Inland energy consumption 20X1 and 20X9

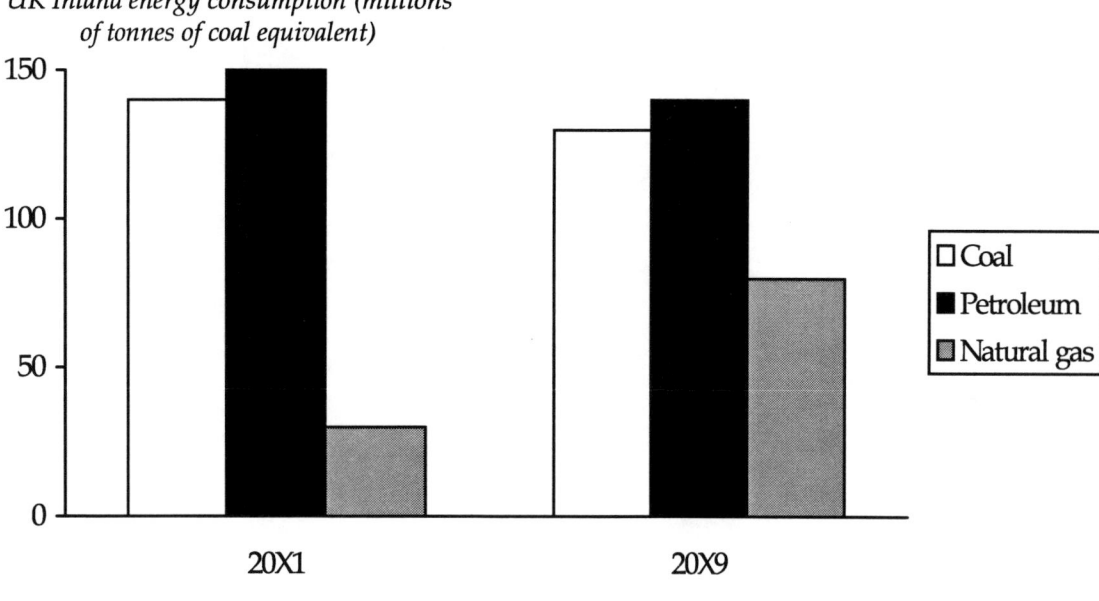

The benefits of the diagrams are:

(1)   (a) shows total energy consumption for each year but (b) does not.

(2)   (b) allows us to use a larger vertical scale than (a), giving increased accuracy.

(3)   (b) shows the trend or change between the years for each energy product.   [(a) also shows this trend but not as clearly.]

6   **BTC**

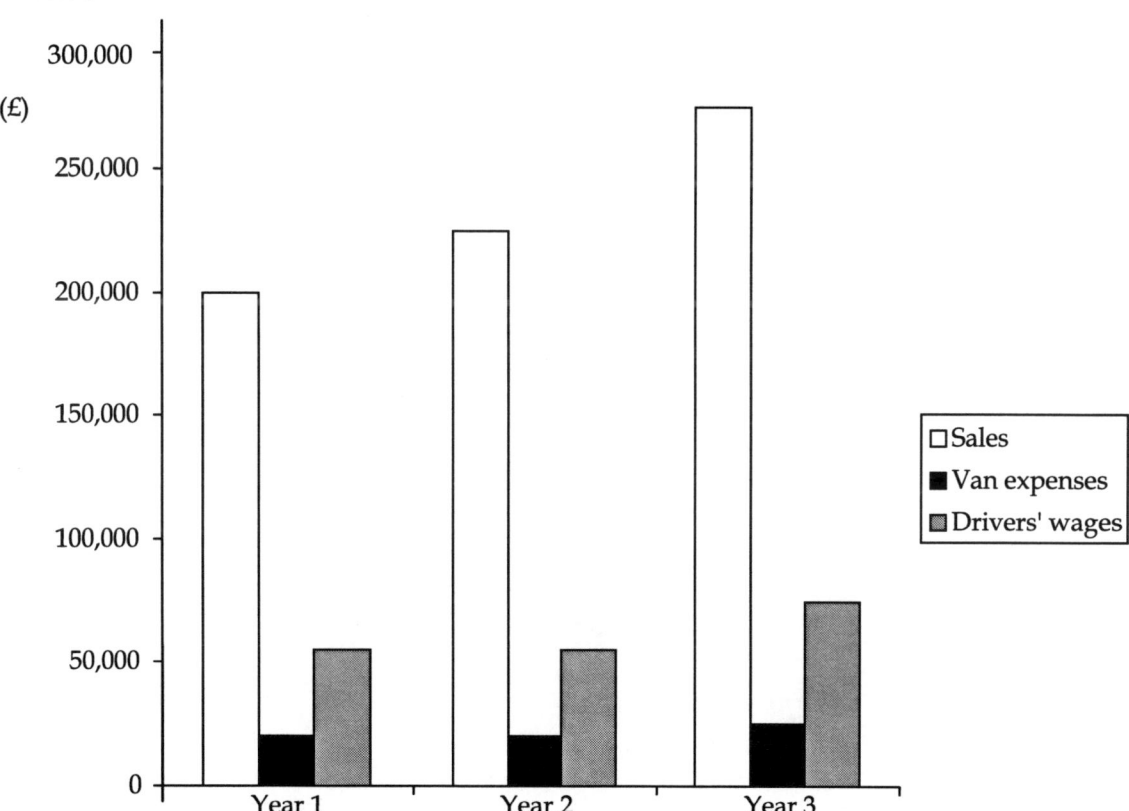

Chapter 4

1   Video v DVD

(a)   Graph of number (in millions) of video recorder/players sold.

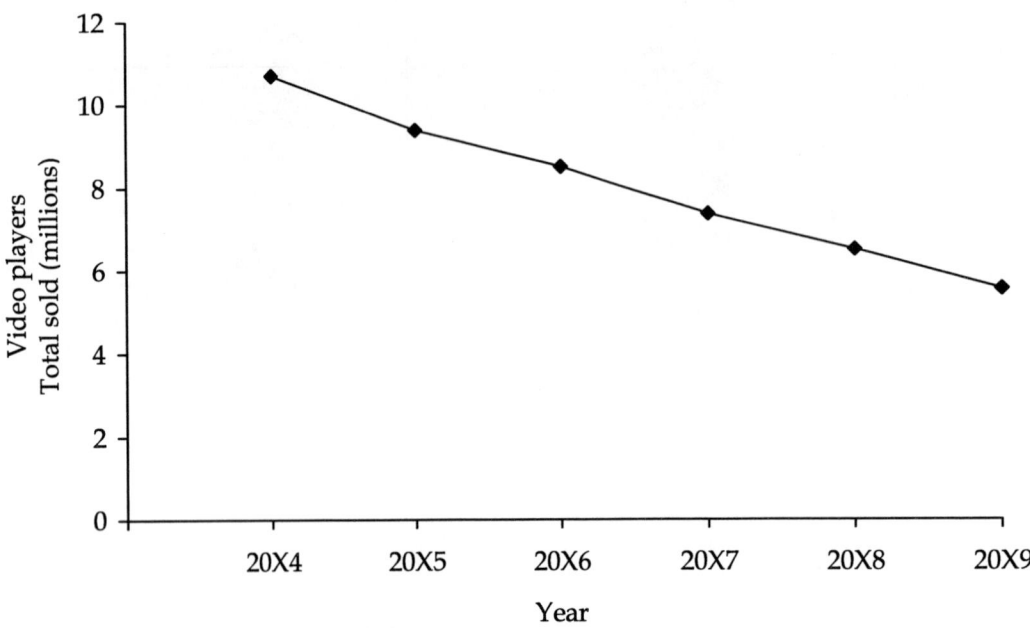

The graph shows that there has been a regular decline in the number of video players sold over the period. The data follows an almost perfect straight line.

(b)   The best way of answering this question is to find the total number of players sold each year and plot this on a graph.

Year	20X4	20X5	20X6	20X7	20X8	20X9
Sales (millions)	17.43	17.67	18.00	18.09	18.49	18.27

As the graph indicates, the total number of players sold increased fairly steadily up to 20X8, then fell again in 20X9. Thus it would appear that up to 20X8 the fall in sales of video players was compensated by an increase in sales of DVD players.

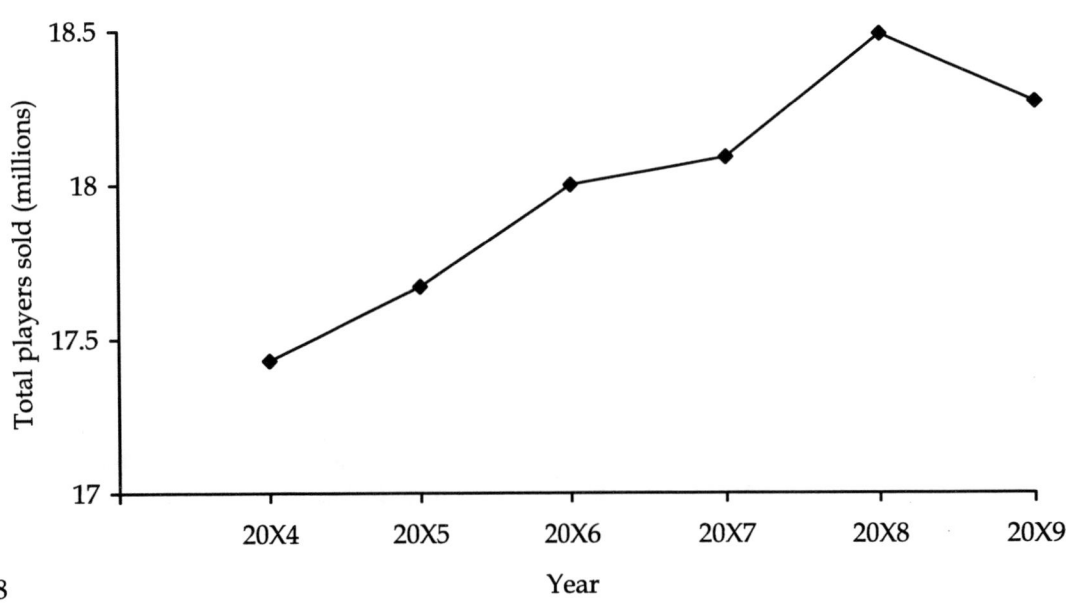

2   Trends

    1   is seasonal

    2   is a trend

    3   is probably (arguably) cyclical

    4   is random

To rank these trend, seasonal, cyclical, random would mean:

2, 1, 3, 4 (answer B)

3   Moving averages

£	Three-year total £	Three-year moving average £
100		
110	318	106
108	330	110
112	327	109
107		

4   Movements

The characteristic movements (or components) of a time series are as follows:

(1)   **The basic trend** is the general direction in which the graph of a time series appears to be going over a long interval of time. The trend may be represented on the graph of the times series as a smooth curve or in special cases by a straight line.

(2)   **Seasonal fluctuations** are the identical, or almost identical, patterns which a time series follows during corresponding intervals of successive periods. Such movements are due to recurring events such as the sudden increase in department store sales before Christmas. Although, in general, seasonal movements refer to a period of one year, this is not always the case and periods of days, hours, weeks, months, etc., may also be considered depending on the type of data available.

(3)   **Cyclical variations** refer to long term oscillations or swings about the trend line or curve. These cycles may or may not be periodic, ie they do not necessarily follow exactly similar patterns after equal intervals of time. In business and economic situations movements are said to be cyclical if they recur after time intervals of more than one year. A good example is the trade cycle representing intervals of prosperity, recession, depression and recovery.

(4)   **Random variations** are the sporadic motions of time series due to chance events such as floods, strikes, elections, etc. Although it is ordinarily assumed that such events produce variations lasting only a short time it is conceivable that they may be so intense as to result in new cyclical or other movement.

For the situations listed the following are the main characteristic movements with which they would be associated:

(i)   random variation;

(ii)   cyclical variation;

(iii)   seasonal variation;

(iv)   trend;

(v)   seasonal variation;

(vi)   cyclical variation;

(vii)   seasonal variation;

(viii) trend;

(ix)   random variation;

(x)   trend.

5   **WBA**

20X4	Quantity	Price	Pence
Cover	1	10.6p	10.6
Paper	230	31p/100	71.3
Ink	5	1p	5
Binding	1	3p	3
			89.9

$$\text{Index} = \frac{89.9}{86.8} \times 100 = 103.6$$

6   **Energy supplies**

(a)

Year	Sales revenue £	Calculation £	Deflated sales revenue £
20X1	486,000	486,000 × 111.8/111.8	486,000
20X2	521,000	521,000 × 111.8/131.9	441,606
20X3	562,000	562,000 × 111.8/145.9	430,648
20X4	604,000	604,000 × 111.8/150.3	449,283
20X5	683,000	683,000 × 111.8/156.3	488,544

(b)   When the increase in the RPI is taken out of the figures it can be seen that until 20X4 sales revenue was in fact falling and that it is not until 20X5 that sales revenue in real terms rises above the 20X1 level.

Chapter 5

1 **Haulage accounting unit**

(a) Tonne/mile or tonne/kilo

(b) Client hour charged

(c) Bed day; patient

2 **The Snowy Ski Company**

(a)

	Week 1	Week 2	Week 3	Week 4
Total Actual Hours				
South Wales	16,582	18,860	20,070	19,226
Yorkshire	14,270	15,121	16,910	15,597
Ski Units Completed				
South Wales	1,200	1,350	1,400	1,300
Yorkshire	1,000	1,050	1,150	1,100
Hours per unit				
South Wales	13.8	14.0	14.3	14.8
Yorkshire	14.3	14.4	14.7	14.2

(b) REPORT

To: Mr O'Hagan

From: An Accounting Technician

Subject: The efficiency of the South Wales and Yorkshire Factories

---

Performance was analysed over a four week period.

With the exception of week 4 the South Wales factory was consistently more efficient than the Yorkshire factory, generally taking 3 per cent fewer hours overall to produce one ski unit. However, it should be pointed out that this 3 per cent may not be significant if there are cost differences between the two factories, or indeed differences in equipment used.

The Yorkshire factory's actual labour hours also generally exceeded standard hours produced, the only exceptions being the Moulding Department in week 2, the Assembly Department in week 1 and the Finishing Department in week 4.

The South Wales factory worked well in weeks 1 and 2 with overall favourable variances, but adverse variances for Moulding (week 1) and Finishing (week 2). Week 3 saw an overall adverse variance caused by a very high adverse variance in the finishing department. Week 4, however, saw extremely serious problems with large adverse variances in all departments.

Clearly the large adverse variances require some explanation throughout, however, some measure of significance is required to judge which variances are large. 5 per cent of budget may be a suitable figure in this case.

In particular, the very high adverse variances in week 4 in South Wales require explanation. Was there a power failure or machine breakdown? Have labour conditions changed, or is there a regular monthly cycle of this nature?

An explanation is also required into why Yorkshire seems to be relatively consistently worse than South Wales. Is it reasonable that the same budgeted labour hours apply to both factories or are conditions in each slightly different? Are the standards set in the Yorkshire factory correct or is the training regime different in Yorkshire?

The figures alone are insufficient to judge the overall performance of the factories. Qualitative information is also necessary.

3   Business Computers Ltd

Task 1

Business Computers Ltd
Table of ratios

Division	Ratio	20X4	20X5
Hardware – Commercial	Net profit/sales	17.5%	14.8%
	Development costs/sales	34.7%	40.0%
	Sales per employee	£22,107	£19,202
Hardware – Government	Net profit/sales	36.6%	35.5%
	Development costs/sales	30.9%	31.6%
	Sales per employee	£41,200	£40,804
Software & Consultancy	Net profit/sales	39.4%	48.5%
	Development costs/sales	21.7%	18.8%
	Sales per employee	£23,614	£26,875

Task 2

Business Computers Ltd
Report on Divisional Performance

To:	Financial Accountant
From:	A Technician
Date:	18 June 20X6

The revenue for the Hardware Commercial division in 20X5 has declined from 20X4 as has the net profit/sales ratios. The development costs have risen and the sales per employee gone down.

Overall the results of the Hardware Commercial Department are alarming as each indicator is worse in 20X5 than in 20X4. The increase in the development/sales ratio and the decrease in the sales per employee show there is a pressure upon costs whilst the ability of staff to generate revenue is decreasing. This seems to be reflective of the increasingly changing and competitive nature of the market the company operates in.

The revenue for the Hardware Government division has declined in 20X5, as has the net profit/sales ratio slightly. The development costs over sales have increased and the sales per employee have gone down slightly. Overall the results for 20X5 are disappointing compared to 20X4, however, the changes are not as severe as the Hardware Commercial Department. Also analysis must be tempered by two factors; firstly that government spending restrictions might have cut back performance and secondly this division can be seen to act as a loss leader for the innovative software and consultancy division.

The Software and Consultancy division has had a good year. Sales are up, as is the net profit/sales ratio, development costs per sales are down and there is a marked improvement in sales per employee. The indicators are good but could they have been better?

Overall the company should concentrate upon the hardware government division which is connected to the highly profitable Software and Consultancy division. Long term prospects also look good given government intentions. Looking at the financial data, the company should keep only a nominal presence in the Hardware Commercial market.

4   Grand Hotel Group

Task 1

		20X0	20X1	20X2
(a)	Net profit (£)	220,000	10,000	460,000
(b)	Net profit %	6.9%	0.3%	12.8%
(c)	Average staff costs (£)	5,143	5,231	5,739
(d)	Turnover at year 1 prices (£)	3,200,000	2,719,626	3,243,243

Report to the directors on recent financial trends

Net profit has moved from £220,000 in 20X0 to £10,000 in 20X1 through to a figure of £460,000 in 20X2. The net profit ratio has moved from 6.9% of sales in 20X0 through to a negligible 0.3% in 20X1 and on to a 12.8% net profit in 20X2.

The implementation of the programme does seem to have had a very beneficial effect upon profitability in 20X2. This can partly be explained by the fact that fixed costs seem to be recovered and any pricing policy above marginal cost will add to profit.

Average staff costs have moved gradually up from 20X0/X1 whilst there is nearly a 10% jump in 20X2 on the 20X1 figure (£5,231 to £5,739). It does seem that the rise in 20X1 might have initially been caused by a lack of control over labour costs and then maybe by higher rates for full-time employees for 20X2.

Sales in real terms have increased. The increase in sales in real terms in 20X2 compared with 20X0 is commendable given that average disposal income has fallen over the period and the unemployment rate has increased.

Task 2

Report to the directors on ratio analysis within the Grand Hotel Group

(a)	Total revenue	20X0	20X1	20X2
	Room occupancy %	64.8%	60.3%	80.6%
	Revenue per employee	£22,857	£22,385	£31,304
	Profit before fixed charges as a percentage of revenue	63.1%	62.2%	60.0%
	Average revenue per room let	£113	£110	£102

The programme does seem to have met its objectives as total revenue in 20X2 has increased by 24% over 20X1 and the net profit percentage has moved upwards to 13%. Also, whilst room occupancy fell from 64.8% in 20X0 to 60.3% in 20X1, it rose to 80.6% in 20X2.

Sales activity has increased in 20X2 whilst revenue per room has decreased, reflecting discounted tariffs. There appears to be a more efficient utilisation of staff as, whilst their basic rates have increased by just over 11% between 20X0 and 20X2, the sales per employee have gone up from £22,857 in 20X0 to £31,304 in 20X2.

Fixed costs have gone down by £100,000 which has increased profitability in 20X2. This could have been brought about by decreasing administration overheads. The profit before fixed charges as a percentage of revenue has declined from 63.1% in 20X2 to 62.2% in 20X1 and 60.0% in 20X2. This seems to be caused by the competitive pricing policy which had led to an increase in sales as stated above.

(b)   Additional useful information which could be provided includes the following:

-     How is the hotel competing against industry average?
-     What is the performance compared with budget?
-     Information about how staff have adapted to change
-     Information about perception of services by customer
-     What are the results of the individual hotels?
-     Break-down of revenue and costs for rooms and food and beverages

5   BTC

Task 1

Years	1	2	3
Sales (£)	200,000	202,000	199,000
Van expenses (£)	14,000	14,423	16,981
As percentage of sales	7	7.1	8.5
Drivers' wages (£)	52,000	56,600	68,150
As percentage of sales	26	28	34.2
Number of vans	3	3	4
Sales per van (£)	66,667	67,333	49,750
Number of deliveries	1,000	1,100	1,400
Sales per delivery (£)	200	183.6	142.1

Task 2

To: General Manager

From: Assistant Accountant

Subject: Transport operation   **Date**: June 20X4

Section 1

(Note Appendixes 1 and 2 are in the question and are not added to this report.)

1.1   In Appendix 1, attached to this report, are details of sales and main cost items relating to the above operation. 'Key ratios' have been calculated to assist in interpreting the performance.

1.2   Most of the 'key ratios' have improved: sales have increased and van expenses are down from 7% to 6.6% of sales, drivers' wages have similarly reduced from 26% to 25% and the number of deliveries has increased. The only hiccup is in the sales per van for year 3. However, as the new van was purchased during the year, a full year's use was not achieved.

1.3   On the basis of Appendix 1, the operation is working efficiently.

Section 2

2.1   In Appendix 2, also attached to this report, the same 'key ratios' were calculated and a different picture emerged. The reason for the difference from Appendix 1 is that specific price rises have been removed from the figures.

2.2   Sales have hardly changed during the three years. Van expenses and drivers' wages have both increased as a percentage of sales. Sales per van have fallen, indicating that the utilisation of vans is not as good as it used to be. The new 'key ratio' of sales per delivery is interesting as it indicates that smaller deliveries are being made than previously.

2.3   On the basis of Appendix 2, the operation is not working as efficiently as in year 1.

Section 3

3.1   The transport operation is not as efficient now as it used to be. There is a need to control van expenses and drivers' wages carefully. The fall in sales per delivery could mean that customers are ordering less (although sales have remained steady) or that we are not as efficient in planning our deliveries as we were. Did we need to buy the new van? Static sales could mean a lack of future potential in this sector.

3.2   I believe that, in the future, information of this nature should be produced regularly, at least monthly. Appendix 2 is the model that we should follow as it indicates the underlying quantity changes. One extra 'key ratio' that should be studied is miles per gallon achieved by the vans. This would indicate whether the vans were being efficiently maintained and driven and would also provide a deterrent to anyone attempting to steal petrol.

3.3   This report indicates areas that need investigation.

Chapter 6

1   NTL plc

Task 1

Toy Manufacturer's Trade Association
Inter-firm comparison report, Quarter to 30 September 20X3

	Most profitable	*Average*	*NTL plc*
Direct materials as a percentage of sales	46.9	52.6	55.3
Direct labour as a percentage of sales	10.4	10.1	12.3
Production overheads as a percentage of sales	14.0	16.9	16.6
Production cost as a percentage of sales	71.3	79.6	84.2
Distribution and marketing as a percentage of sales	4.9	3.8	2.9
Administration as a percentage of sales	5.6	5.7	6.8
Net profit as a percentage of sales	18.2	10.9	6.1
Net profit as a percentage of capital employed	40.4	22.6	16.2
Current ratio (current assets to current liabilities)	2.2 to 1	1.9 to 1	1.7 to 1
Quick ratio (debtors to current liabilities)	1.1 to 1	0.9 to 1	0.6 to 1

Task 2

To: Managing Director, NTL plc

From: Admin. Assistant, Toy Manufacturers' Trade Association

Subject: Inter-firm ratios   **Date:** December 20X3

(1)   The comparison report for the last quarter has been completed and is attached to this report.

(2)   NTL plc has not had a good quarter. Its ROCE is below the average and well below the 'best' company.

(3)   Profit to sales is poor and the biggest influence is production cost. Both material and labour costs are high and an examination of the buying policy and grade of labour employed should be undertaken. Scrap rates and labour efficiency should also be studied.

(4)   A significant ratio is that of distribution and marketing to sales. This is rather low and could indicate that more effort and resources need to be committed to marketing.

(5)   If an increase in sales could be achieved, then the production overheads and administration overheads ratios could both improve. Certain costs in these areas have to be incurred irrespective of activity achieved.

(6)   The financial ratios give some cause for concern. The current ratio indicates that it may be difficult to finance working capital in the near future. The quick ratio is worrying because NTL plc is not able to pay its short-term debts at the moment.

(7)   If the bank is not prepared to increase the overdraft, then another source of finance needs to be found. There is a need to control stocks and to retain profits within the company. This matter needs immediate attention.

Task 3

(a)   **Re-worked trading and profit and loss account for quarter to 30 September 20X3**

	£	£	£
Sales			718,300
Materials		397,220	
Labour		88,351	
Variable production overheads	35,924		
Fixed production overheads	75,740		
		111,664	
Production cost			597,235
Distribution and marketing (fixed)			18,937
Advertising campaign (fixed)			20,000
Administration (fixed)			44,404
Total cost			680,576
Net profit			37,724

(b)

To:	Managing Director	
From:	Admin. Assistant	Ref:
Subject:	Proposed advertising campaign	**Date:** 3 December 20X3

(1)   The marketing area was mentioned in my previous report as one which should be expanded. The suggestion of an advertising campaign is to be welcomed.

(2)   The purpose of the campaign is to increase sales, which it is expected to do, but it is essential that profits also should be increased. The re-worked accounts (Appendix 1) indicate that profits would be reduced.

(3)   The proposed campaign is thus not acceptable but it needs to be reconsidered, not necessarily abandoned. Alternative proposals should be discussed with the major aim being to increase profits.

(4)   Before commencing any campaign, it is important that funds are available.

Chapter 7

1

	£
Output VAT	
Standard rated (22,400 × 17.5%)	3,920.00
Zero rated	-
	3,920.00
Less: input VAT (16,300 × 17.5%)	2,852.50
VAT due to Customs and Excise	1,067.50

Chapter 8

1

	£
List price	380.00
Less: trade discount 10%	38.00
	342.00

VAT   =   £342.00 × 96% × 17.5%

      =   £57.45

2   (a)

Quantity	Description and price	Net of VAT	VAT rate	VAT
16	6 metre hosepipes @ £3.23	51.68	17.5%	9.04
24	12 metre hosepipes @ £5.78	138.72	17.5%	24.28

    (b)   VAT = £1,084.50 × 17.5%

               = £189.78

3   VAT = £68.90 × 17.5/117.5

            = £10.26

4   (i)   15 July actual tax point

    (ii)   12 August actual tax point

    (iii)   4 September actual tax point

    (iv)   13 September basic tax point

Chapter 9

1 Panther

The two basic records needed are the sales day book and purchase day book for the sales and purchases.

For cash sales and purchases the cash book should be analysed.

Information about credit notes received and issued should be in the purchase returns and sales returns day books.

The capital goods purchased and sold will probably be in a separate assets account under plant and machinery unless the company maintains analysed purchase and sales day books which include asset purchases and disposals.

The goods taken for own use should be recorded in the sales day book and the drawings account.

The bad debt relief is generally found in the bad and doubtful debts account.

2

(a)   **VAT account 1 January to 31 March 20X1**

	£		£
VAT on purchases	1,422.30	VAT on sales	2,709.98
EC acquisitions	117.08	EC acquisitions	117.08
	1,539.38		2,827.06
Less: credit notes received	163.70	Less: credit notes issued	284.50
Total tax deductible	1,375.68	Total tax payable	2,542.56
		Less: total tax deductible	1,375.68
		Payable to Customs and Excise	1,166.88

Value Added Tax Return
For the period

1/1/X1 to 31/3/X1

For Official Use

Registration number	Period
285 3745 12	01X1

┌─────────────────┐
Long Supplies Ltd
Vale House
Lily Road
Trent
TR5 2KL
└─────────────────┘

Your VAT Office telephone number is 0123-4567

You could be liable to a financial penalty if your completed return and all the VAT payable are not received by the due date.

Due date: 30 April 20X1

For Official Use	

Before you fill in this form please read the notes on the back and the VAT Leaflet *'Filling in your VAT return'*. Fill in all boxes clearly in ink and write 'none' where necessary. Don't put a dash or leave any box blank If there are no pence write '00' in the pence column. Do not enter more than one amount in any box.

For official use				
	VAT due in this period on sales and other outputs	1	2,425	48
	VAT due in this period on acquisitions from other EC Member states	2	117	08
	Total VAT due (the sum of boxes 1 and 2)	3	2.542	56
	VAT reclaimed in this period on purchases and other inputs (including acquisitions from the EC)	4	1,375	68
	Net VAT to be paid to Customs or reclaimed by you (Difference between boxes 3 and 4)	5	1,166	88
	Total value of sales and all other outputs excluding any VAT. Include your box 8 figure.	6	15,251	00
	Total value of purchases and all other inputs excluding any VAT. Include your box 9 figure.	7	8,761	00
	Total value of all supplies of goods and related services excluding any VAT to other EC Member States.	8	None	00
	Total value of all supplies of goods and related services excluding any VAT, from other EC Member States.	9	669	00

Retail schemes. If you have used any of the schemes in the period covered by this return, enter the relevant letter(s) in this box.

If you are enclosing a payment please tick this box	DECLARATION You or someone on your behalf must sign below.
✓	I .... declare that the information given (Full name of signatory in BLOCK LETTERS) above is true and complete. Signature .... Date 20 **A false declaration can result in prosecution.**

Workings

Box 1	£
VAT on sales	2,709.98
Less: VAT on credit notes	(284.50)
	2,425.48

Box 4	£
VAT on purchases	1,422.30
EC Member States acquisitions	117.08
	1,539.38
Less: VAT on credit notes	(163.70)
	1,375.68

Box 6	£
Standard rated sales	15,485.60
Zero rated sales	1,497.56
	16,983.16
Less: credit notes	
Standard rated	(1,625.77)
Zero rated	(106.59)
	15,250.80

Box 7	£
Standard rated purchases	8,127.45
Zero rated purchases	980.57
EC acquisitions	669.04
	9,777.06
Less: credit notes	
Standard rated	(935.47)
Zero rated	(80.40)
	8,761.19

Index

Exam Text Review Form

AAT UNIT 7 TEXTBOOK – PREPARING REPORTS AND RETURNS

We hope that you have found this Text stimulating and useful and that you now feel confident and well-prepared for your examinations.

We would be grateful if you could take a few moments to complete the questionnaire below, so we can assess how well our material meets your needs. There's a prize for four lucky students who fill in one of these forms from across the Syllabus range and are lucky enough to be selected!

	Excellent	*Adequate*	*Poor*
Depth and breadth of technical coverage			
Appropriateness of coverage to examination			
Presentation			
Level of accuracy			

Did you spot any errors or ambiguities? Please let us have the details below.

Page	Error

Thank you for your feedback.

Please return this form to:

The Financial Training Company Limited
Unit 22J
Wincombe Business Park
Shaftesbury
Dorset SP7 9QJ

Student's name: ....

Address: ....

....

....